Praise for

Dare to Be True

"Every page of this book will challenge you to inspect your daily commitment to truth telling and will prompt you to examine your style of truth telling. Give truth a chance to work in your life. *Dare to Be True* will show you how."

—HUGH HEWITT, author, columnist, and radio host
of the nationally syndicated *Hugh Hewitt Show*

"The relationship between truth and a healthy Christian life never struck me so forcefully as when I read *Dare to Be True*. Without getting bogged down in a quagmire of ethical dilemmas and uncertainties, Mark Roberts tackles the daunting challenge of being authentic in an age of spin and contrived images. I doubt if there is any man or woman who would not benefit from this book's encouragement to speak and live the truth."

—CHUCK SMITH, JR., senior pastor of Capo Beach Calvary
and author of *Epiphany: Discover the Delight of God's Word*

"*Dare to Be True* is a crucial compass for anyone who seeks to be a person of integrity in a world where it's very easy to lose your way. Mark Roberts not only discerns the contours of today's perilous moral landscape; he shows us the practical steps we can take to live in the direction we long to go in our finest moments. In contrast to the platitudes about character that are common these days, this book is jam-packed with illustrations that show that the author understands the complexity of the life we live and how it can be truer in all the best ways. This book is an invaluable guide for any individual, family, or group eager to go farther on the adventure of authentic growth."

—DANIEL MEYER, senior pastor of Christ Church of Oak Brook

"Mark Roberts's new book needs to be read right now. He lays bare the 'truth tyrants' of our society and offers an illumination of truth that can enhance every relationship in our lives. This book is full of grace and truth."

—RONALD C. WHITE, JR., historian and author

of *Lincoln's Greatest Speech*

DARE TO BE
TRUE

MARK D. ROBERTS

DARE TO BE
TRUE

LIVING *in the* FREEDOM *of* COMPLETE HONESTY

WATERBROOK
PRESS

DARE TO BE TRUE
PUBLISHED BY WATERBROOK PRESS
2375 Telstar Drive, Suite 160
Colorado Springs, Colorado 80920
A division of Random House, Inc.

Italics in Scripture quotations reflect the author's added emphasis.

The author has made every effort to ensure the truthfulness of the stories and anecdotes in this book. In a few instances, names and identifying details have been changed to protect the privacy of the persons involved.

ISBN 1-57856-704-1

Published in association with Yates & Yates, LLP, Attorneys and Counselors, Orange, California.

Library of Congress Cataloging-in-Publication Data
Roberts, Mark D.
   Dare to be true : living in the freedom of complete honesty / Mark D. Roberts—1st ed.
      p. cm.
   ISBN 1-57856-704-1
   1. Truthfulness and falsehood—Religious aspects—Christianity. 2. Christian life—Presbyterian authors.
I. Title.
BV4627.F3R63 2003
241'673—dc21   2003012046

Printed in the United States of America
2003—First Edition

10 9 8 7 6 5 4 3 2 1

To my mother, Martha Roberts,
who always told me to tell the truth
and who taught me to be truthful by her consistent honesty.

CONTENTS

FOREWORD

In describing the death of truth in his day, Isaiah lamented, "Truth stumbles in the public square, and honesty finds no place there" (Isaiah 59:14, TEV). Sadly, Isaiah could be talking about our culture today. All around us truth has been sidelined in favor of tolerance or political correctness. People are afraid to speak the truth, and many even express doubts that there is such a thing as "truth." "What may be truth for you," they say, "may not be truth for me." I have even heard followers of Jesus make that absurd assertion.

In an age of moral relativism and ethical ambiguity, I cannot think of a more needed corrective than the one given in this book. Mark Roberts has written a tract for our times, a brilliant explanation of the essential importance of truth in every area of our lives. His goal for us is the same as *The Living Bible's* paraphrase of Ephesians 4:15: "We will lovingly follow the truth at all times—speaking truly, dealing truly, living truly—and so become more and more in every way like Christ who is the Head of his body, the Church." It takes truth to transform us, and spiritual growth is the process of replacing the lies in our lives with truth. That's why Jesus prayed, "Sanctify them by the truth; your word is truth" (John 17:17, NIV).

When you get to chapter 6, "Truthful Community," you will find that it's worth the price of this book. Cultivating real community takes honesty, which is lacking in most relationships. You have to care enough to lovingly speak the truth to others, even when you would rather gloss over a problem or ignore an issue. While it is much easier to remain silent when those around us are harming themselves or others with a sinful pattern, it is not the loving thing to do. Most people have no one in their lives who loves them enough to tell them the truth, so they continue in self-destructive ways.

Often we know what needs to be said to someone, but our fears prevent us from saying anything. Many Christian fellowships have been sabotaged by fear: No one had the courage to speak up while a member's life fell apart. That's why we desperately need this book. It shows us how to be *people of the truth*.

It is my passionate prayer that God will use this book to save thousands of relationships, marriages, small groups, and churches from the destructive damage of dishonesty. If you want to move beyond superficial relationships and develop real fellowship with other believers, study this book with others, then put the principles into practice, because there is no community without candor! May God bless you.

—RICK WARREN, author of *The Purpose-Driven Life* and *The Purpose-Driven Church*

ACKNOWLEDGMENTS

Once again I want to thank the team of people who have helped turn this book from a dream into a reality: Ron Lee, my editor at WaterBrook Press; Don Pape, my publisher; the helpful staff at WaterBrook; Sealy Yates and Curtis Yates of Yates and Yates, LLP, my literary agents and consistent encouragers.

I am indebted once more to my faithful congregation at Irvine Presbyterian Church. Many of their stories fill these pages, reflecting their willingness to join me on the journey of discipleship. I am especially thankful for my ministry colleagues, both staff members and elders, and for my "think-tank" partners in the Pastor's Study.

How grateful I am for those who regularly encourage me in my writing: Hugh Hewitt, Buddy Owens, Milt Jantzen, and my covenant group partners.

I also want to acknowledge the hospitality of my friends at the Newport Beach Athletic Club and Tully's Coffee in Irvine. Lots of good work gets done while I'm churning away on the elliptical trainer or enjoying the best latte in town. In fact, this book was first conceived during a conversation at Tully's.

As always, I thank God for my dear family, Linda, Nathan, and Kara. Your support, patience, and love keep me going. You're the best!

Finally, I want to acknowledge my parents, who taught me in word and deed what honesty was all about. This book is dedicated to my mother in gratitude for her tireless efforts to help me become a truthful person.

DO YOU DARE?

The Challenge and Promise of Truthfulness

Y es, it's like, I know I'm lying, but it's just gonna make my life so much easier."[1] So confessed the popular young actress Tara Reid, star of such cinematic classics as *Josie and the Pussycats*, in a magazine interview. The context for the interview? Reid's pending testimony in the assault trial of a close friend accused of ramming her car into a group of sixteen people.

It's easy to condemn Tara Reid's readiness to lie. We could smugly conclude that it's typical of pampered celebrities to shove ethics aside for the sake of self-interest. But we must at least admire the ironic truthfulness of Reid's confession. Most liars just lie. They don't announce it in advance.

The esteemed accountants of Arthur Andersen, for example, didn't warn Enron stockholders to run for cover because company losses were about to be disguised as financial gains. There was no cautionary announcement, just financial reports that deceived thousands of people, including many who staked their retirement investments on the trustworthiness of Arthur Andersen's word. If Tara Reid had been an accountant rather than an actress, at least she might have tipped off the credulous investors in advance of Enron's collapse.

The Life of Complete Honesty

Before we look down our noses at pampered starlets and greedy corporate execs, we might first check to see if our own noses are growing like Pinocchio's. Though we prefer to think of ourselves as honest people, many of us have honed the skill of deception, often without realizing it. No matter what we *believe* about lying, our actions at times adhere to the unspoken credo that lying does in fact make life easier.

Well, you might be thinking, *narcissistic actresses might live by that credo, but not me!* Really? What do you say when your husband asks if his suit still fits? The objective truth is, "Sure, if you don't mind a ring of fat hanging pendulously over your belt!" But how do you actually answer his question?

Or let's say your wife greets you at the door with "How do you like my new hairstyle?" As soon as you see her, your mind becomes a television screen showing Wile E. Coyote with his finger in an electrical outlet, every hair standing at shocked attention. As you pull the plug on your mental picture, how do you answer your wife's question?

Here's a tougher one. What words flow from your lips when you eagerly open a birthday gift from your young child, only to feast your eyes on the ugliest necktie or cheesiest piece of costume jewelry known to modern civilization?

It could be argued that a lack of complete honesty in these situations is harmless, even kind. What good purpose is served by hurting your loved ones with the unvarnished truth? This is an astute question, especially given the hurt that is caused by the tactless comments of people who spout out whatever enters their minds. Sometimes they even defend their rudeness by claiming that they are simply being honest. That's not what I mean by "complete honesty."

A life of complete honesty is one that is filled with truth, so much so that there is no room left for falsehood. Being fully honest has nothing to do with brazen frankness that brutalizes others. Instead, it is an all-encompassing integration of thoughts, words, and actions, so that outward expressions follow truly from what's in your heart. Complete honesty means speaking the truth while at the same time living by the truth of love's preeminence. (In a later chapter we'll take a close look at situations in which forthright speech could bruise another's feelings.)

For most of us, the struggle of truthful living is not that we're tempted to be too honest, but rather, not honest enough. We're attracted to words and actions that promise ease, comfort, and convenience. If these goals are achieved through some minor truth twisting, then it's easy to justify the use of a strategic half-truth. And once it's justified, we're on the road to a lifestyle of deception.

Here's a common situation that invites deception. You've been under a lot of pressure at work. Your boss has been hassling you about missing deadlines and not staying on top of your accounts. You've been working extra hours and doing everything you can to prove that you can handle the job. Suddenly you realize that you were supposed to be at an important meeting with a key account ten minutes ago. What do you say when you show up late? Do you blame the traffic that you knew in advance would slow you down? Do you mention the phone call that you easily could have terminated sooner if you had only chosen to do so? Do you play fast and loose with the facts, hoping your client will see you as a victim of circumstances and not as simply irresponsible? Or do you honestly acknowledge that you failed to take the steps necessary to arrive on time, hoping that your boss won't reprimand you for once again making an important client wait? How often, in the daily course of events, do you truthfully take responsibility for things that might put you in a bad light?

We all face tough challenges like this on a regular basis. For example, what should I have said a few years ago when my six-year-old son asked innocently, "Dad, what *did* President Clinton lie about?" That was as good a time as any to join the former president in truth twisting, don't you think? Or what should a man from my church have said when asked by his perennially cranky boss, "So how do you like working in my department?" A truthful "I hate it" wouldn't have contributed to job security.

Ironically, Tara Reid was telling the truth. Sometimes lying *does* make things easier.

The Pervasiveness of Lying

People throughout our society follow the convenience-over-truthfulness credo. We all can point to infamous—and blatant—examples of lying. The president of the United States stares into the television camera and lies about his extramarital affair. The chair of the U.S. Olympic Committee resigns because of falsehoods in her résumé. The rest of us don't capture headlines, but we also bend the truth to the point of breaking, often without recognizing it.

A recent study of 2.6 million job applicants found that 44 percent of all résumés contain not just minor exaggerations, but outright lies.[2] In a survey of teenagers, 92 percent admitted to lying to their parents in the last year. Seventy-eight percent lied to their teachers. And these are just the ones who recognized the lie and admitted their dishonesty.[3] Dr. Robert Burton, writing on the prevalence of duplicity in the medical profession, commented, "Lying is everywhere; it is as intrinsic to daily life as any search for truth."[4]

A study conducted by Professor Robert Feldman of the University of Massachusetts found lying to be more common than anticipated. In his study, pairs of strangers were put together for ten minutes and instructed to carry on a conversation. They were unaware that their conversations were being videotaped. Afterward, as the participants viewed the tape, they were asked to indicate anything they had said that was not true. Sixty percent admitted to telling at least one lie. The average person lied more than twice—and this was during only ten minutes of casual chitchat!

Feldman concluded, "People tell a considerable number of lies in everyday conversation. It was a very surprising result. We didn't expect lying to be such a common part of daily life." The participants also were shocked by their own deceptive behavior. "When they were watching themselves on videotape, people found [that they had lied] much more than they thought they had," Feldman observed.[5]

If you and I had participated in this study, we might well have had the same sort of eye-opening experience. At least *I* might have. When I began writing this book, I started to scrutinize my own behavior. I was amazed—you might even say horrified—by how often I was tempted to lie and by how often I *did* lie before I could stop myself. For instance, seeing an old friend, I said, "Oh, it's good to see you. I've been thinking about you so much recently." In truth, I had thought about this friend for only a fleeting moment a few days before our chance meeting. But "so much" was more than an exaggeration. It was a lie that slipped out before I could catch it.

I know I'm not the only one who does this. I preached a series of sermons on truth to my congregation. Over the course of four months, members of my church examined their own conversations. Many shared how stunned they were to discover that they often compromised the truth. Some were led to confront deeply embedded habits of deception. I hasten to add that these folk are committed, mature Christians. But some found it all too easy to say things such as "I've been praying for you" when they really hadn't been. Others discovered that their excuses for declining an unwanted invitation left truth in the dust. "I'm sorry, I have another engagement" sounded so much better than "I really prefer not to have dinner with you." Some people had become so accustomed to truth twisting that they didn't even recognize the tendency until they shone the piercing light of Scripture upon their lives.

Lying pervades our society and sometimes even our own lives. If during the next few days you pay close attention to your interactions with others, odds are that you also will find yourself struggling to be fully honest. Even if you're not tempted to tell baldfaced lies, you may find yourself engaging in the widespread—and widely accepted—practice of spin.

Snared by Spin

Bill Press, former host of CNN's *Crossfire* and author of the book *Spin This! All the Ways We Don't Tell the Truth,* refers to our era as "the Age of Spin." What is spin? Press explains:

> There is no good definition of spin. It's easier to say what it's not than what it is: It's not the truth. Neither is it a lie. Spin lies somewhere in between: almost telling the truth, but not quite; bending the truth to make things look as good—or as bad—as possible; painting things in the best possible—or worst possible—light.[6]

As a major league pitcher puts spin on a curve ball to confuse a batter, so the verbal spinner twists the truth to keep the listener off balance. Spin involves saying things that are true in some sense, but not speaking the full truth that ought to be spoken. It can lead to out-and-out lying, though it is usually more subtle and therefore potentially more pernicious. When we spin the facts, we can excuse our lack of truthfulness or even congratulate ourselves on our cleverness.

We may never see a clearer demonstration of spin than what goes on in the quadrennial presidential debates. One candidate rolls out an impressive list of "indisputable" facts upon which to base grandiose claims about his presidential qualifications. Then the other candidate presents an equally impressive collection of facts that contradict everything the previous speaker just claimed. The first candidate then appears to commend his opponent while at the same time implying that he is a rank liar. Returning the favor, the second candidate lectures the first on the evils of making personal accusations and claims the moral high ground, while at the same time insinuating that his opponent is a lying scoundrel. And so it goes for ninety minutes.

The spin factor of the debates themselves is nothing compared with the postdebate commentary. Immediately after the candidates conclude, their spin doctors start performing radical surgery on reality. Their message: "Our candidate had a commanding grasp of the issues, far better than anyone expected and obviously way ahead of his opponent." This message is spun with ebullience no matter how the candidate performed. The one who stumbled over his words will be praised as "thoughtful rather than hasty and superficial, like his opponent." The one who exaggerated his record will be lauded as "a bold visionary, just the opposite of his unimaginative adversary." If a candidate were to spend the entire debate drooling all over his shirt, his campaign director would exult afterward, "America is ready for a *real* person in the White House, a person we can relate to. We're tired of someone with a dry mouth and all the answers. We want a president who is genuine enough to let the world see him drool."

Whether or not we're in the midst of an election year, we can't escape spin. Advertisers spin their products. Coaches spin their losses. Students spin their low grades. Spouses spin their marital messes. Corporate executives spin their bottom lines. Employees spin their mistakes.

Maybe you think you're immune. And *maybe* you are. But most of us, when we examine our behavior, find that we can spin with the best of them.

For example, when my high-school friend Mike first received his driver's license, his mother allowed him to use her car but forbade him to drive on the freeway. Of course, Mike and I were convinced that we knew better than his mother. We were teenagers, after all. So we bravely challenged the Southern California freeways. Knowing that his mother might question us about Mike's driving, however, we crafted a brilliant spin on our behavior.

Sure enough, after one of our illicit road trips, Mike's mom asked him bluntly, "Mike, did you drive on the freeway today?"

Without hesitation and with a hurt tone in his voice, Mike answered, "Mom, I know the rules. Of course I drove on the surface streets." As he spoke, I nodded fervently. (Mike *did* know the rules and we *had* driven on the surface streets—on our way to the freeway.) The combination of Mike's earnest testimony and my bobbing head duped Mike's mom, who apologized for questioning his integrity.

Mike and I didn't tell an outright lie, but we did fabricate a deceptive half-truth. This was spin, pure and simple, because we intended to mislead, while failing to confess the truth that deserved to be spoken. Mike and I were spin doctors in training—and Mike avoided losing his driving privileges.

Have you ever put a spin on the truth for the sake of self-promotion or self-protection, and, in the process, failed to say what you really should have said? Let me encourage you to put down this book and take a few minutes to scrutinize your recent behavior. Ask the Holy Spirit to help you remember. Did you promise to pray for someone, knowing that you'd probably forget your vow ten minutes after making it? Did you choose your words too carefully in explaining a situation at work so you could avoid taking the blame for something you messed up? Did you mislead a friend, an employee, your boss, your spouse, or maybe even yourself? Think about it.

THE WAGES OF SPIN

If everybody spins, then maybe we shouldn't lose sleep over it. After all, a little finessing of the facts does seem to make life easier.

Although some of the spin that surrounds us appears to be innocuous (we all know that a certain brand of shampoo doesn't really send women into ecstasy), I'm convinced that the wages of spin are insidious. Consider the implications of what Mike and I told his mother. Although she never discovered our deception, if she had she would have trusted us far less (and rightly so), both for our disobedience and for our dishonesty. Spin breeds suspicion. It *damages trust* and therefore *undermines healthy relationships.*[7]

This sorry result of spin plagues our nation. According to a recent poll, the vast majority of Americans don't trust the government. Eighty percent of respondents agreed: "Government leaders tell us what they think will get them elected, not what they really believe."[8] Consider your own response to the presidential debates every four years. Do you really believe what the candidates are saying? Do you fully trust even your favorite candidate?

The private sector is not immune. According to one analyst of American business practices, "The proliferation of spin is like a top out of control. The more people spin, the worse the situation becomes through erosion of trust and breeding of skepticism."[9] Widespread cynicism is also directed toward the news media and even the church. For months my heart would break as every day the headlines announced new allegations leveled against the Catholic clergy. But accusations of molesting children were only part of the problem. The scandal was multiplied tenfold by the deceptions employed by church officials to protect the offending priests. According to a recent Gallup poll, trust in the church has hit a record low.[10] And if we Protestants think we're free from such problems, we're fooling ourselves. I can't tell you how many times I've spoken with people who are new to my church, only to hear of their disillusionment with the church in general because of the deceptions they've experienced. When clergy across the denominational spectrum misuse sex, money, or power, we often resort to lying in order to cover up our abuses.

Both spin and its turbocharged cousin, unabashed lying, pummel our most precious relationships. As a pastor I've seen husbands and wives assault their marriages through deception. A husband invests some retirement savings in a risky business venture without consulting his wife. When she inquires about oddities in their financial statements, he covers his actions with a veneer of half-truths. But when his wife discovers what is really happening, she wonders if she'll ever be able to trust her husband again. Or a man discovers that all the time his wife was "sending e-mail to her friends," she was, in fact, conducting an online affair with a stranger she met in a chat room. Marriages are shredded by the jagged edges of deceit.

Similar devastation is visited upon parent-child relationships. I've seen dozens of teenagers squander their parents' trust by lying. When the school's vice principal calls home to inquire about a student's multiple absences, the parents discover they have been duped. Trust crumbles and familial love is stretched to the limit.

But parents can also be the source of deception. As I began working on this book, I discovered some distressing things about myself. For example, when I have the freedom to spend an evening at home, I often escape to my study, where I focus on preparing sermons or writing. Somewhere around 8 P.M. my eight-year-old daughter, Kara, will interrupt me with a simple request. "Daddy, can you come tuck me in now?" My response is usually something like, "Sure, just a minute." But, I'm ashamed to admit, that minute is sometimes more like ten minutes, or twenty, or even more. There have been times when I was so wrapped up in my work that I completely forgot my promise to come in "just a minute."

Even though I wasn't intending to lie, my failure to be truthful could damage my relationship with my daughter. Over time Kara could easily begin to wonder, "When Daddy says something, can I believe him? Can I trust him?"

Our failure to be truthful injures not only our dearest human relationships but also our most priceless relationship of all, our relationship with God. Since God is the Source of all truth, embracing falsehood means we turn our backs on God.

The Rewards of Truthfulness

Once we tally up the negative costs of deceit, including loss of trust, growing cynicism, and shattered relationships, we'll be inclined to leave dishonesty in the dust. Then, if we calculate the riches earned by truthful living, we'll begin to feel the powerful attraction of being truthful.

Just as deceit breeds doubt and disease in our relationships, truth generates trust and health. If we are truthful, we will earn the trust of those who mean the most to us, and this trust will lead to sound relationships. Mutual truthfulness invites you to let down your guard and be yourself. Although speaking openly sometimes incites momentary conflict, when it is done in love, it almost always produces deeper community. Truthfulness breaks through the superficiality that limits intimacy and personal growth.

Living in complete honesty affects not just our relationships but also our personal well-being. Lies, even so-called white lies, weaken our moral fortitude. As ethicist Sissela Bok observes in her classic study of lying, "After the first lies...others can come more easily. Psychological barriers wear down; lies seem more necessary, less reprehensible; the ability to make moral distinctions can coarsen."[11] Conversely, habitual truthfulness strengthens our moral resolve. Honesty in relatively insignificant matters prepares us to tell the truth when much more is at stake. And in practicing the habit of truthfulness, we experience in dramatic ways the rich rewards of consistently living the truth.

Truthfulness also leads to personal freedom. Some of us feel the heavy burden of our own deceit. We hate it and yearn to unload it. Even those who have become so used to falsehood that they no longer sense its oppression are nevertheless imprisoned by it. Subsequent lies are called into service to prop up the first one. And who has enough memory cells to keep track of what was said to whom? Keeping it all straight is exhausting. Truthful living, in contrast, offers freedom from guilt, denial, and stunted personal growth. It means we don't have to waste energy pretending to be someone we're not. In a passage from the gospel of John, Jesus makes a stirring promise, "You are truly my disciples if you keep obeying my teachings. And you will know the truth, and the truth will set you free" (John 8:31-32). We can enjoy freedom by knowing and doing the truth. It's the very real freedom that comes from living authentically, without ever feeling the need to hide.

Truth, then, enhances the level of trust in our most important relationships. It brings the riches of personal freedom to our daily lives. But the rewards don't end there. Perhaps the most precious result of truthful living is deeper intimacy with our truthful God. It includes confronting parts of ourselves that we'd much rather avoid, thus leading to reconciliation with God. When we reject deception and speak the truth instead, we honor the God who calls us to truthfulness and honesty. Our obedience pleases God, and we sense his joy and pleasure in us. But, even more profoundly, when we live truthfully, we imitate God. We become more like what God intended us to be as human beings created in his image. We live life more fully and more freely.

Dare to Be True

So, you may be thinking, *I'm convinced. Truthful living, here I come!* Your intentions are laudable, but aren't you forgetting something? Remember the ironic wisdom of Tara Reid: Lying is often so much easier. In a spin-drenched world where deception is a given, truthful living is not only difficult, it's costly. And sometimes it's excruciating.

The challenge of truthfulness isn't new, however. Four centuries before Tara Reid touted the benefits of lying, the English poet George Herbert wrote,

> Lie not; but let thy heart be true to God,
> Thy mouth to it, thy actions to them both:
> Cowards tell lies, and those that fear the rod;
> The stormy working soul spits lies and froth.
>> Dare to be true. Nothing can need a lie:
>> A fault, which needs it most, grows two thereby.[12]

Even in seventeenth-century Britain, truthfulness required not just dedication, but daring; not just conviction, but courage. Cowards, unwilling to tackle the challenge of honesty, told lies. Sounds familiar, doesn't it?

Strangely, George Herbert agrees with Tara Reid's basic premise, but he disagrees with her conclusion. Yes, lying is easier, Herbert acknowledges, but telling the truth is better, even if it's harder. "Dare to be true," he urges us. Don't sell out to the easy deceitfulness of this world, but choose instead the truthfulness of God.

In his wisdom Herbert counsels us not merely to tell the truth, but to *be true*. It's a matter not just of words, but of our entire being. Truthfulness begins when our hearts are "true to God." Ultimately, it must govern both our mouths and our actions. This kind of pervasive truthfulness requires commitment and, indeed, courage.

Truthfulness also depends upon a transforming encounter with God, the Author of truth. Try as we may, we will have neither the daring nor the desire to be true unless God first transforms our hearts. Ultimately, our penchant for falsehood flows from the sinfulness of our souls. But the good news is this: God is in the heart-renovating business. The Truthful One who desires "honesty from the heart" will teach us to be wise in our "inmost being" (Psalm 51:6). God will answer if we cry out to him:

> Teach me your ways, O LORD,
>> that I may live according to your truth!
> Grant me purity of heart,
>> that I may honor you. (Psalm 86:11)

Daring to be true must begin with God. Before we start trying to tell the truth, let alone daring to live in complete honesty, we must face God, the Truthful Trinity. If we are willing to approach God on his own terms, we will come to a deeper understanding of the truth and how to let it fill our lives. Moreover, we will discover a God who will cheer us on in our efforts to live truthfully.

As a being created in the image of God, you were made for truthful living. You will be your true self, you will live the fullest life, you will find the peace that your heart seeks only when you reject the lie and choose the truth. No matter how much you have been tainted by deception, the deepest part of your being yearns for truth, to know God in truth, and to live in truth each day. The road to truth may be tortuous and less traveled, but it is the only road that will bring you to your true home.

May this book be a map to guide you there!

THE TRUTHFUL TRINITY

THE TRUTH YOU CAN TRUST

I once served on a committee that helped prepare people for pastoral ministry. When church members sensed God's calling, we would help them clarify that calling and prepare for the rigors of seminary education. Among the pastors and lay leaders on the committee, one member had singularly impressive academic credentials. Dr. Robert Adams was the chair of the philosophy department at UCLA, one of the most highly touted philosophy departments in the world. Though a brilliant philosopher, Dr. Adams was also a kind Christian man who always encouraged ministerial candidates and never flaunted his brilliance.

One day our committee met with a young man barely out of college. Ted was bursting with enthusiasm but lacking in experience. He had earned only average grades in college, while pursuing a narrow course of studies. The committee was concerned that Ted would be overwhelmed by the demands of seminary. Because he was young and his education was limited, we hoped to persuade him to take a few college classes in the humanities before moving on to graduate school.

Dr. Adams volunteered to handle this rather delicate assignment. He began graciously, complimenting Ted on his obvious commitment to Christ. Then Dr. Adams moved to the issue of Ted's educational background.

"We're a little concerned," he began, "with the narrowness of your academic record. Usually we like to see a broader range of subjects in a candidate's transcript."

"I don't understand," Ted objected. "There's nothing wrong with my record."

Gently, Dr. Adams continued. "We're not saying there's anything wrong with what you have accomplished. But we would like you to consider taking a few more classes, especially in the humanities, before you go to seminary."

"The humanities!" Ted groaned. "Are you talking about marshmallow classes like philosophy and stuff?"

"Well," replied the distinguished professor of philosophy, "yes, I was thinking about classes like 'philosophy and stuff.' But, to tell you the truth, I'm not sure I would characterize them as 'marshmallow' classes."

Rather flippantly, Ted responded, "Oh, I never thought those things mattered. That's why I didn't study them."

Talk about an awkward moment. My stomach was in a knot, but Dr. Adams took the conversation in stride. While the dignified professor remained gracious, I wanted to shout to Ted: "You numskull! Do you have any idea what you're talking about or with whom you're talking?" I wish I could have been part of the conversation when somebody finally told Ted what Dr. Adams did for a living. (That conversation did take place, and a penitent Ted did indeed take a few college classes before entering seminary.)

Although I was ready to put Ted in a headlock because of his presumptuousness, now I must acknowledge a bit of my own presumptuousness in writing a book on truth. *This* is no marshmallow topic! It's one of the most profound and controversial subjects of all. In fact, you might want to ask me the same question I was itching to ask Ted: "Do you have *any* idea what you're talking about?"

I don't claim to be an expert, but over the years I've gained some familiarity with this complex subject. As an undergraduate I majored in philosophy, taking a number of courses that dealt with the nature of truth. My professors argued that truth is simply a human construct, that there is no absolute truth apart from human perception and language. They never reached a consensus on the nature of truth, and philosophers still debate the issue. So, yes, I am aware that I'm tackling a complex and contentious subject. Unlike Ted, however, I am approaching this conversation well aware of my limitations.

But there's an even more compelling reason for humility in such a discussion. When we talk about truth in any absolute sense, we can't help but confront the very nature of God. In fact, God is present in our conversation both as a subject and as an active participant. When we talk about truth, we're standing on holy ground. Even as Ted should have been humble in the presence of a renowned philosopher, so should we remember our place when discussing truth in the presence of the One who is the Truth.

TRUTH AND THE NATURE OF GOD

Truth is a bigger issue than any of us can fathom. It's nothing less than an essential aspect of God's nature. Because God is Truth, there is no truth apart from God. When we read the Bible, we can't help but confront the fact that God and truth are inseparable. There is a necessary interrelationship between the two.

Before diving into a practical discussion of truth and its implications for daily life, we must examine the Source of truth. If we were to jump ahead without first exploring the interrelationship between God and truth, we would miss the most important aspect of truthful living. As you encounter God, who reveals himself as the Truthful Trinity, you will find that your motivation to become a person of truth grows geometrically. The more clearly you see God, the more you will yearn to be like him.

The Old Testament God of Truth

In the Hebrew Scriptures, God and truth hang together like twins connected at the hip. To separate them would be to damage both. Notice, for example, the words Moses used to celebrate God's greatness: "He is the Rock, his work is perfect: for all his ways are judgment: a *God of truth* and without iniquity, just and right is he" (Deuteronomy 32:4, KJV). Similarly, David cries out, "[R]edeem me, O LORD, the God of truth" (Psalm 31:5, NIV). It follows from God's truthful nature that his "words are truth" (2 Samuel 7:28). What God declares is accurate. What he promises will occur. It makes sense that God is completely honest, having no partnership with falsehood.

Consider the words of God himself, spoken through the prophet Isaiah:

I did not speak in secret,
  in a land of darkness;
I did not say to the offspring of Jacob,
  "Seek me in chaos."
I the LORD speak the truth,
  I declare what is right. (Isaiah 45:19, NRSV)

This striking text speaks as incisively today as it did centuries ago. Our postmodern world resembles a land of darkness where people stumble without the light of God. Rejecting divine revelation, many walk in chaos and confusion. How desperately we need to hear not only that God is truth but also that he has revealed himself to us in a way we can understand. We can be set free from the intellectual, moral, and spiritual chaos that typifies our culture because we can know the God of truth.

The Truthful Trinity in the New Testament

The New Testament maintains and builds upon the Old Testament notion of God's truthfulness. Whoever accepts the testimony of Jesus must acknowledge that "God is true" (John 3:33). But truthfulness relates not only to God the Father. Jesus is the Word of God made flesh, "full of grace and truth" (John 1:14, NRSV). Jesus himself boldly stated, "I am the way, the truth, and the life. No one can come to the Father except through me" (John 14:6). As the Word of God, Jesus embodies divine truth, revealing all that is necessary for eternal life. Indeed, he becomes the way through which we receive eternal life.

Yet the New Testament expands still more our understanding of truth. The truthfulness of God pervades the character not only of the Father and the Son but also of the Holy Spirit, the third member of the Trinity. To his disciples Jesus explained, "When the Spirit of truth comes, he will guide you into all truth. He will not be presenting his own ideas; he will be telling you what he has heard" (John 16:13). The Holy Spirit has been sent by Jesus from his heavenly Father to deliver the truth of God.[1] Thus, in the New Testament we meet the Truthful Trinity. The Father, Son, and Holy Spirit personify truth, speak the truth, and work together to draw us into a truthful relationship with the triune God.

A CALL TO HUMILITY

If you regularly pursue theological inquiry, you might be thinking this is all old hat. But if you're like most people I know, you're feeling a bit flummoxed. Though you believe that God is triune, you find discussions of the Trinity to be perplexing and, frankly, humbling.

Stay with that feeling! There is perhaps no sentiment more appropriate than humility as we stand before the God of truth. The mystery of the Trinity reminds us that, although we know God truly, we are not the masters of truth. God is the sole Master. Therefore, as we dare to be true in daily living, we must do so with humble hearts.

My friend Jeff is a theologically trained, intellectually gifted Christian who cares deeply about the truth. He can also set new records for arrogance when he's talking about it. In theological conversations Jeff sometimes dispenses his version of the truth as if he were God giving the Law to Moses on Mount Sinai. When others disagree with him, they are simply wrong. No further discussion is needed. Every now and then I have asked Jeff, "So, do you think there's even a *tiny* possibility that you might be wrong?" He begrudgingly allows for that possibility, as long as it's a microscopic possibility.

Truth tyrants like Jeff alienate Christians and secularists alike. They forget that "God sets himself against the proud, but he shows favor to the humble" (James 4:6). Moreover, they forget the One who is the Source and Lord of all truth. How can we strut about proudly as masters of the truth when we must rely so utterly on God's gracious revelation if we are to know the truth at all? We need sincere gratitude for the truth, not smug ownership of it.

Christians have full access to the God of truth, but that doesn't mean we've cornered the market on this commodity. Scripture frequently reminds us that our knowledge of God is imperfect. The psalmist announced, "How great is our Lord! His power is absolute! His understanding is beyond comprehension!" (Psalm 147:5). When Job repeatedly demanded an accounting from the Lord for his suffering, God finally spoke: "Who is this that questions my wisdom with such ignorant words? Brace yourself, because I have some questions for you, and you must answer them. Where were you when I laid the foundations of the earth? Tell me, if you know so much" (Job 38:2-4). Then God continued for four chapters to remind Job of just how little he knew about God's nature and power.

Yes, Christians have the privilege of knowing God and his truth. But we also must acknowledge that divine truth transcends our limited experience, language, and knowledge. Though we can know many true things about God, we cannot *fully* know the infinite, holy, perfect God of truth this side of heaven.

As I call for humility in the face of truth, I find myself in ironic agreement with postmodernism. During the era of modernism, humans were so optimistic about the power of the mind that we sought to master the truth through human reason and the scientific method. Postmodern thinkers see things differently. They have realized that, no matter how hard we try, no matter how advanced our technology, we will *never* be able to claim full mastery of truth. As Christians we agree with this conclusion, recognizing that God alone is the Master of truth and that his truth always transcends our understanding.

Yet this does not mean, as some postmodernists claim, that we can never know absolute truth with confidence. We believe that God, the Truthful Trinity, stands outside of human perception and that truth, therefore, is absolute, transcending human limitations. Moreover, we understand that God made us with the capacity to grasp transcendent truth, however incompletely. God has revealed ultimate truth in a manner we can fathom through Jesus Christ, through Scripture, and through the truth-teaching ministry of the Holy Spirit.

But this raises another question: Can we trust God's revelation? Or, even more pointedly, can we trust God? These questions bring us back to Scripture, to a consideration of the nature of truth.

TRUTH THAT EARNS OUR TRUST

Throughout the Bible, truth is not some abstract intellectual ideal. Rather, it is a down-to-earth relational reality. Think of the way different Bible translations render the Hebrew word for *truth* as it relates to God. Where the original language states, literally, "God of truth," translators vary between "God of truth" and "faithful God."[2] This variation accurately captures the complexity of the Hebrew word *'emet,* which means both "truth" and "faithfulness."[3] It either describes a situation where a statement mirrors reality, or it describes a person who acts faithfully.[4] This latter sense of *'emet* frequently expresses God's own reliability, as in Exodus 34:6: "I am the LORD, I am the LORD, the merciful and gracious God. I am slow to anger and rich in unfailing love and *faithfulness.*" In this context, *'emet* is God's utter steadfastness in relationship with his people. Thus, when the Old Testament speaks of God's truthfulness, both his accuracy in speech and his steadfastness in relationship are signified.

The underlying sense of the Hebrew word *'emet* is "reliability" or "firmness." A statement is true if it is solid enough to support belief. People are faithful if they can be counted on. In both cases, *'emet* merits trust. If people speak truly and act faithfully, then you can put your weight upon them, so to speak. That's the reliability and firmness of truth in the dynamic of a relationship.

Throughout the Old Testament God reveals himself as one who can be trusted in word and deed. Because God is truthful, he doesn't lie and he is also utterly reliable. We can trust him completely.

Although New Testament writers use the Greek vocabulary for truth, the Old Testament notion of truth as faithfulness hovers nearby. Jesus explained that the "Spirit of truth...will guide you into all truth" and is therefore trustworthy (John 16:13). Because God "cannot lie," we can have "confidence" in his promise of eternal life (Titus 1:2). In the book of Revelation, the risen Christ identifies himself as "the Amen—the faithful and true witness" (3:14). Therefore, we can place our trust in God, who is both full of truth and a reliable guide to truth.

In traditional weddings a century ago, grooms and brides said to each other,

"I pledge thee my troth." The word *troth* is closely related to the word *truth*. Both stem from the Old English term *trēowth*. Troth is good faith or fidelity. By pledging his troth to his bride, the groom claimed to tell the truth as he made his vows. But even more, he was promising to be faithful to her "as long as we both shall live." He was saying, "I can be trusted. You can count on me."

According to Scripture, the God of *'emet* is both truth-full and troth-full. God speaks accurately, without lying. God also acts faithfully, without failing. Thus we can believe what God reveals, and we can put full confidence in what he promises. We can trust his word, and we can trust him with our very lives.

TRUSTING THE GOD OF TRUTH

When I think of trusting the God of truth, I immediately picture Ron and Erin Hesse. They are mission partners of my church, serving in Indonesia with Wycliffe Bible Translators. Ron and Erin are so committed to the truth of God that they have devoted their lives to translating the Bible into Tehit, a language into which Scripture has never before been translated.

But Ron and Erin's commitment to God's truth is inseparable from their trust in the God of truth. Leaving behind the comforts of America, they moved to a small rural village in Indonesia to live among the Tehit people. There they are raising four children in spite of dangers most of us would consider unacceptable. The plentiful poisonous snakes of the jungle have now been joined by transplanted Al Qaeda terrorists. But the Hesses remain surprisingly calm—they are not naive about the risks they face, but they are also utterly confident in God's faithfulness. Ron and Erin, who have dedicated their lives to translating God's *'emet*, have confidence that the God of *'emet* is completely trustworthy.

The Hesses' example challenges me because, frankly, I often struggle to trust God. For some strange reason I seem to think I can do a better job of running the universe than God can. When situations don't work out as I want them to, I wonder if God is faithful. I worry about what will happen to my life, my family, and my church. But then, by grace, I'm drawn once again to the Scriptures. I'm reminded that God's faithfulness is great, that his mercies are new every morning, that his unfailing love never ends (see Lamentations 3:22-23). I remember how utterly reliable God has been in my life. Not that he's done everything according to my plans, to be sure. But I see once again that God's ways are best, even if I can't fully fathom them. With the apostle Paul my heart proclaims, "Oh, what a wonderful God we have! How great are his riches and wisdom and knowledge! How impossible it is for us to understand his decisions and his methods!" (Romans 11:33).

LIVING IN LIGHT OF THE TRUTHFUL TRINITY

We have already seen that the nature of God as the Truthful Trinity instills both humility and trust within us. Before I draw this chapter to a close, I want to consider three additional practical implications of God's absolute truth and his truthful nature.

1. *It's all right to contradict the world's assumptions about truth.* It's common-place these days to hear that there is no such thing as absolute truth. The more we hear this, the more uncomfortable we might become regarding our own convictions. We may even feel the need to apologize for adhering to the idea of absolute truth. But we need to recognize two things: First, where truth is involved, apologies are never needed; and, second, we should fully expect that our stand on truth will differ from the world's view.

If you were to audit the average college philosophy course, you would hear truth described as a lofty ideal we can never attain, as a figment of the human imagination, or as an accident of human language. Increasingly, truth is re-duced to a cultural construct, something relative to and limited by one partic-ular culture. As a white male American Christian from Southern California, for example, I have my version of truth. Those from other cultures have their dis-tinct versions. No view of truth should be considered more or less valid because truth itself is relative. There is no "higher truth" that transcends human cul-ture and creativity.

This view of truth can be quite upsetting. During my undergraduate stud-ies in philosophy, I often wondered why my brilliant professors conceived of truth in terms so contradictory to my own. Sometimes my wonder turned to worry. Was there really transcendent truth as I'd always thought, or had I been dead wrong?

Given what we see about truth in the Scriptures, we need not be distressed when secular views differ widely from our own. When people discuss truth as if God were either nonexistent or nonessential, their conclusions will have little in common with the insights derived from Scripture. Remove God from the truth equation, and your solution will necessarily be relative, transient, and unreliable.

I'm not suggesting that we should never study secular philosophy, however. As disciples of Jesus we have been set apart by God to be his representatives in the world.[5] If we seek to communicate with the people to whom we have been sent, then we must learn their language, just as Ron and Erin Hesse have learned the language of the Tehit people. In particular, we must grapple with other views of truth. But we should not be troubled when we discover that our ideas are fundamentally out of sync with those of our nonbelieving neighbor. A profound difference between Christian and secular views of truth is exactly what we should expect.

2. *Since God is Truth, all truth is of God.* As a college freshman I took my first university-level class in the Bible. The professor was a wise, articulate scholar whose knowledge of the New Testament impressed me, just as many of his opinions distressed me. He contradicted assumptions I had made about the New Testament, and he backed up his views with persuasive evidence. Though he didn't deny traditional faith in Christ, he was skeptical about the extent to which such faith could be based on Scripture. By the end of the term, I found myself doubting the truthfulness of the Bible. I hesitated to examine my doubts too closely, however, because I was afraid that serious inquiry would further undermine my faith.

I'm not the first Christian to have had such an experience, and I'm not the last. Most of us encounter ideas that contradict the fundamental tenets of our faith. When this happens, some Christians begin to worry that serious study undercuts serious faith. They discourage intellectual investigation, preferring what they call "simple faith." Out of fear, they stop seeking truth and instead bury their heads in the sand of rigid ideology or misty-eyed sentimentality.

I can understand this reaction because I have sometimes wanted to keep my own intellect safely disengaged. During that college Bible course I began to wonder if I should dispense with the academic study of the Bible. Yet I realized I would never be satisfied if I suspected my faith was intellectually untenable. Still, I feared that my quest for historical truth would chip away at my belief.

Then God provided help in the form of Dr. John Stott. A highly respected Christian thinker and expert in the New Testament, Dr. Stott visited Harvard in the latter part of my freshman year. A friend hosted an informal dessert gathering and invited me to attend. Here was my chance to talk with someone who could understand my dilemma.

When another student finished a conversation, I finally had my chance. "Dr. Stott," I said, "I'm taking a New Testament class, and much of what I'm being taught contradicts what I believe about the Bible. I'm beginning to wonder if it's unwise to study Scripture in an academic way. I'd like to take more classes in New Testament, yet I'm afraid that what I learn will undermine my faith. What do you think I should do?"

"I can understand your conflict and your fear," Dr. Stott began, "because I've felt them myself. Many of the popular theories in New Testament scholarship do challenge orthodox Christianity."

"But," he continued, "you don't have to be afraid. Let me tell you something that will give you confidence as you study: All truth is God's truth. There isn't anything true about the Bible that God doesn't already know. You don't have to fear that if you dig too deeply you'll undermine genuine Christian faith. You may indeed discover that some of your beliefs aren't correct. In fact, I hope you do make this discovery many times over. That's what happens when you live under biblical authority. But you never have to be afraid of seeking the genuine truth because all truth is God's truth."

With John Stott's encouragement, I began a lifelong journey of seeking the truth about Scripture. I did indeed take more New Testament classes, ultimately earning a Ph.D. in this field. I came to see that much of what I was being taught in that introductory course reflected the skeptical, antisupernatu-ralistic assumptions of my professor, not the data of the New Testament itself.

Yet, throughout my years at Harvard, I also learned a great deal from that professor. Although we often differed on essential matters, he showed me that I did not have all the truth. I had so much to learn, even from one who thought quite differently from me.

Because *all* truth is God's truth, there is much truth to be found outside orthodox Christian theology. Sometimes well-intentioned believers feel com-pelled to reject any knowledge that cannot be derived from Scripture. They argue that there can be no truth outside of Christian doctrine, that all other religions and philosophies are completely false. Yet this argument fails to do jus-tice to the breadth of divine truth. Such an orthodox theologian as John Calvin once wrote,

> Therefore, in reading profane authors, the admirable light of truth dis-
> played in them should remind us, that the human mind, however much
> fallen and perverted from its original integrity, is still adorned and
> invested with admirable gifts from its Creator. If we reflect that the Spirit
> of God is the only fountain of truth, we will be careful, as we would
> avoid offering insult to him, not to reject or condemn truth wherever it
> appears. In despising the gifts, we insult the Giver.[6]

Even "profane authors," secular philosophies, and religions outside the Judeo-Christian tradition can affirm genuine truth. We can learn from these, know-ing that wherever genuine truth appears—whether in science or philosophy or religion—it still finds its ultimate source in God.

We need the freedom of knowing that all truth is God's truth, since we live in a multicultural world that bombards us with multifaceted truths. When I was in elementary school, religious diversity meant that there were Methodists and Catholics in my class. Last year, in my son's second-grade class, there were Muslims, Buddhists, Hindus, and Jews, not to mention Methodists, Catholics, and students who claimed to have no religious affiliation at all. So how do we bear witness to the truth of God in such a diverse world? How do we respond to the religious convictions of others?

One popular approach is to claim that Christianity is completely true and everything else is completely false. This narrow perspective overlooks the fact that we share a large body of truth with Jews, some of which also shows up in Muslim theology. But if all truth is God's truth, then we can affirm genuine truth in religious traditions independent from our own. For example, we can agree with Buddhists that suffering pervades human experience. Yet we disagree over the primary cause of suffering: for Buddhists it is desire; for Christians it is sin.

Practically speaking, we can and should listen sensitively to the religious beliefs and experiences of others. We might even learn something. For instance, although I reject Islamic theology, I have been challenged by the commitment of Muslim people to pray regularly throughout the day. We can be genuinely open to the religious beliefs of others without condoning popular misconceptions, such as the notion that all religions offer equally valid paths to God. As Christians we continue to believe that Jesus is the Truth in a unique way, even if this can seem uncharitable. Truthful religious dialogue must include our faithful yet humble presentation of our Christian convictions, even when they contradict the views of others. Yet if we listen respectfully, if we affirm what is true in the beliefs of others, if we seek to find genuine common ground, and if we listen and speak with humility, then others will listen to us and be drawn to the God of truth who has revealed himself in Jesus. We can be completely honest about our faith without being rude or arrogant.

3. *The Truth seeks us before we seek the truth.* Though we tend to think of truth as an impersonal abstraction, it is, in fact, profoundly personal. Truth inheres in God, in each person of the Trinity. It is revealed in divine words and deeds and, most of all, in the person of Jesus.

Since truth is personal, it cannot be mastered through expertise or mere intellectual exercise. Truth is to be found, not through dispassionate deliberation, but through a personal relationship with the God who has made himself known in Jesus Christ. Certainly, intellectual investigation can help us understand truth more deeply, so long as our thinking is tethered to personal fellowship with the living God. But intellect alone will never enable us to know the truth.

On the other hand, in saying that we know truth in a personal way, I am not reducing it to mere subjectivity. The truth exists on its own and in its own authority outside of our subjective experience. But sometimes Christians reduce the pursuit of truth to the rationalistic study of theology and doctrine. No matter how valuable this approach may be, it is inadequate. When we seek the truth, we are seeking not a body of knowledge or the authoritative final word, but the living God.

Yet God does more than simply make himself known to those who seek him. God is, in fact, the first seeker. Through the prophet Ezekiel, God said, "I myself will search and find my sheep. I will be like a shepherd looking for his scattered flock" (Ezekiel 34:11-12). In three different parables, Jesus illustrated God's predisposition to pursue those who don't yet know him.[7] If truth were impersonal, it would make little sense to speak of it as seeking us. But because truth is inseparable from God, and because God seeks us, we can rejoice in the fact that, even before we seek truth, Truth seeks us. In this sense, truth and relationship are inseparable.

Jesus developed this point in conversation with a woman from Samaria. "True worshipers," he said, "will worship the Father in spirit and in truth. The Father is looking for anyone who will worship him that way" (John 4:23). In order to find people who will worship him in spirit and truth, God has revealed himself definitively through Jesus, the Son of God. And since Jesus is no longer with us in person, both God the Father and God the Son have sent God the Spirit to be with us. The Spirit of truth will teach us everything and, most important, will help us know Jesus as the Truth.

Therefore, if you seek to know the truth, you must first recognize that the Truth is seeking you. You will find truth not ultimately through philosophical investigation or religious pilgrimages, but through intimate fellowship with the Triune God. The good news is that the God of truth desires to have this kind of fellowship with you.[8]

Although this fellowship takes many forms, including prayer, Bible study, and service in the church and the world, Jesus emphasized worship as one of its essential dimensions. When we worship in the power of the Spirit, and when the content of our worship reflects the truth of God's revelation, then God finds us as "true worshipers" (John 4:23). We worship in the fullness of *'emet*, with truth-full words and with troth-full hearts. Moreover, through genuine worship we grow in the knowledge of God, knowledge steeped in the truth of revelation, knowledge that is deeply personal and intimate.

We know God as the Truthful Trinity, the Master of all truth, and the One who calls us to imitate his truthfulness. We turn to this essential calling in the next chapter.

CALLED TO TRUTHFULNESS

DISTINCTIVE LIVING IN AN AGE OF SPIN

In my first weeks of college, I began attending the meetings of a Christian group at one of the finest churches in New England. More than a hundred students from various schools gathered each Sunday for vigorous singing and inspired Bible teaching by the college pastor. I felt drawn to the group for many reasons, not the least of which was that this group seemed to be an oasis of truth in the wasteland of skepticism where I lived all week.

One evening the pastor delivered a stirring message on sharing the gospel with our friends. At the end of his talk, he passed out surveys. This "Religious Interest Survey" featured a series of questions that led up to the clincher: What do you believe about Jesus? The pastor urged us to poll the students in our dorms using the survey. In this way we could easily enter into conversations about our Christian faith. Perhaps we could even help some students become Christians.

After he had finished giving the instructions, the pastor invited questions. I raised my hand and asked, "What's the deadline for getting these surveys back to you?"

He responded with a chuckle, "Oh, don't worry about that. We aren't going to tabulate the results. This is simply a way to get people talking about Jesus."

This answer didn't satisfy me. Nervously, I followed up with another question: "But if we tell people this is a survey, aren't we implying that we actually care about their answers? Is it honest to call this a survey when we're not really surveying what people think?"

"Look," the pastor said with a touch of irritation in his voice, "it's a survey; we're just not tabulating the answers. Lots of businesses and churches do things like this. It's just a good conversation starter. If you don't want to do it, you don't have to."

I didn't take any "surveys" back to campus with me. For that matter, I didn't return again to the meetings of that college group. It seemed that I was being asked to lie for the sake of talking to my friends about Jesus. The goal was admirable enough, but not the means.

Today I'm *still* uncomfortable with the thinking behind that pseudo-survey. In retrospect, I think my judgment was correct, though not my quick departure from the group. I should have met with the college pastor in private and tried again to communicate my concern. Leaving should have been a last resort. But even as an eighteen-year-old, I sensed the wrongness of employing deception in our efforts to share the good news, even if such an approach was commonplace.

Today I'm more convinced than ever that God has set us apart from the world and its ways. Our life of truth is to contrast sharply with the world around us. This high and honorable calling is your calling and it's my calling. It's ours together as the people of God.

Heroic Truthfulness

If you're looking for a hero who is completely sold out to the truth, no matter what the obstacles and no matter what the potential consequences, you need look no further than the apostle Paul. He stood up for uncompromised truth even when such a stand led to imprisonment, physical punishment, and, eventually, to an untimely death. And Paul, like believers today, found himself contending with a culture that was drowning in spin.

Facing the Challenge of First-Century Spin

We sometimes wrongly assume that our age stands above all others in terms of skepticism and the flagrant disregard for God and his truth. If Paul were here, he'd tell you differently.

In the introduction to this book, I quoted political pundit Bill Press, author of *Spin This!* who observes that our world sits squarely in the Age of Spin. He's right, to a point. Surely ours is *an* age of spin, but it's not *the only* one. The Roman world of the first century A.D. also deserves that title. As the earliest Christians sought to preach God's truth, they confronted a spin-drenched society comparable to our own.

Trade and travel thrived amid the peace of the first-century Roman Empire. Among those who took advantage of Roman roads and waterways were wandering philosophers and preachers. Some of these proffered classic wisdom in hopes of improving humanity. But many were out for their own advantage, seeking human praise or simply trying to make a buck. Among these hucksters were the Sophists, notable for their rhetorical skills and dazzling appearance as finely dressed men of learning. They sounded great and looked great, not unlike the slick gurus of our day who sell their wisdom to thousands who are willing to plop down $299 for a weekend seminar. Experts in flattery and verbal manipulation, the first-century Sophists hoodwinked the masses who freely gave both their honor and their money to these con artists.[1]

The apostle Paul had to distinguish himself from those who, with questionable motives, peddled learning. In his first letter to the Thessalonians, for example, Paul emphasized that his ministry was free from "any deceit or impure purposes or trickery" (2:3). Unlike the transient philosophers who frequented the Thessalonian marketplace, "[n]ever once did we try to win you with flattery, as you very well know. And God is our witness that we were not just pretending to be your friends so you would give us money" (2:5).

Sometimes Paul also needed to differentiate himself from so-called Christian preachers who freely adopted the slick Sophist approach. Nowhere is this more obvious than in the letter we know as 2 Corinthians. Paul wrote this letter to refute the deceptive tactics of his theological opponents and to affirm his own commitment to the truth of the gospel.

A bit of background is in order. The apostle Paul founded the Christian community in Corinth, a major city in southern Greece. After eighteen months of fruitful missionary work there, Paul left behind a solid but struggling church. Not long after his departure, a new band of purportedly "Christian" missionaries came to town, intent upon correcting Paul's supposed errors and redirecting Corinthian loyalties. Presenting persuasive letters of recommendation, these self-proclaimed apostles preached with rhetorical flourish. They presented themselves as shining examples of the victorious Christian life. They criticized Paul for being unpolished in speech and unexceptional in appearance. These "super apostles" even disparaged Paul for declining to accept financial support from the Corinthians, something that the new preachers were delighted to do…but only out of love for the Corinthians, they explained.

Most troublesome of all was the failure of these false apostles to preach the full truth about Jesus. Stressing both obedience to the Jewish law and powerful living in light of the Resurrection, they ignored the cross of Christ and its implications. They proclaimed "a different Jesus" and a "different kind of gospel" (2 Corinthians 11:4). Through cunning and trickery, they distorted the truth of God's Word. Their slickness of speech and appearance bewitched immature Christians who were pulled away from their "pure and simple devotion to Christ" (2 Corinthians 11:3). The false apostles were not serving Christ, but their own personal interests. If Paul were writing today, he might very well have accused his opponents of being spin doctors, since they cleverly sold their half-truths through brilliant rhetoric and a well-polished personal image. Paul lived in an age of spin, which had corrupted his beloved church in Corinth.

Paul's Response to Spin

So what did Paul do in this spin-saturated environment? What did he do to help free his Corinthian congregation from the quackery of the spin doctors and to nurse the Christians' theology back to health?

It would have been tempting, of course, for Paul to try to outspin the spinners. But he knew such a strategy would ultimately be self-defeating. Instead, he chose to distinguish himself from the false apostles and the rest of the

Sophists in the Roman world not only in the content of his message but also in the sincerity of his communication: "You see, we are not like those hucksters— and there are many of them—who preach just to make money. We preach God's message with sincerity and with Christ's authority. And we know that the God who sent us is watching us" (2 Corinthians 2:17). Unlike those who preached for personal gain, Paul spoke from pure motivations.

Moreover, the apostle chose to "reject all shameful and underhanded methods. We do not try to trick anyone, and we do not distort the word of God. We tell the truth before God, and all who are honest know that" (2 Corinthians 4:2). Paul rejected empty rhetoric and truth twisting. Instead, he chose to commend himself through "the full disclosure of the truth."[2] Paul told the truth with complete honesty, and he did so using plain speech.

The Risk of Full Disclosure

The essence of Paul's "full disclosure of the truth" was precisely what his Corinthian opponents sought to hide: the unsettling truth of Christ's death and the call to imitate his sacrifice. Paul understood that the message of the Cross was not an attractive one. In an earlier letter to the Corinthians, he explained, "So when we preach that Christ was crucified, the Jews are offended, and the Gentiles say it's all nonsense" (1 Corinthians 1:23). Yet Paul told the whole truth about Christ, even at the risk of having his message rejected as foolishness.

Recognizing that the trustworthy Christian messenger aptly illustrates the message itself, Paul also told the truth about himself, even when it made him look unsophisticated. In the opening chapter of 2 Corinthians, he wrote,

> I think you ought to know, dear brothers and sisters, about the trouble
> we went through in the province of Asia. We were crushed and com-
> pletely overwhelmed, and we thought we would never live through it.
> In fact, we expected to die. But as a result, we learned not to rely on our-
> selves, but on God who can raise the dead. (1:8-9)

How easy it would have been for Paul simply to speak of his laudable reliance upon God without mentioning the dire struggle that led him to this point of faith. Remember that he was writing to a church congregation that already had its doubts. Was Paul really impressive enough to be a genuine apostle? Well, he sure paled in comparison to the flashy false apostles who had just been in town. Nevertheless, Paul's commitment to openness and to the genuine gospel demanded that the full truth be told, even the potentially embarrassing truth of his own personal struggles. Similarly, in the latter portions of 2 Corinthians, Paul chronicled the various punishments and setbacks he had experienced, trusting that his weakness demonstrated the power of God at work through him. By telling the truth about himself, Paul ensured that God received all the glory. After all, it's pretty hard to make yourself look good by recounting times when you were flogged or your prayers weren't answered.[3]

Not Just Truth Telling, But Truth-full-ness

In Paul's life, full disclosure of the truth was a matter not only of speaking but also of daily living. In 2 Corinthians he began to make his case against the spinners by pointing to his behavior—not only his words—both in Corinth and throughout the Roman world: "We can say with confidence and a clear conscience that we have been honest and sincere *in all our dealings*. We have depended on God's grace, not on our own earthly wisdom. That is how *we have acted* toward everyone, and especially toward you" (1:12). Unlike his opponents and contrary to their accusations, Paul had always been completely honest and sincere. What was in his heart was also upon his lips. The Corinthians didn't have to look for hidden meanings and secret motivations.

Paul viewed truth telling as an all-consuming pursuit. It went far deeper than words alone; it required that a person *live* the truth. He exemplified the life that, centuries later, George Herbert commended: "Lie not; but let thy heart be true to God, / thy mouth to it, thy actions to them both."[4] Paul was truthful—a quality he defined by living a life that was filled with truth. Truth-full-ness comprises not only what we say, but what we treasure in our hearts and how we act in the world. It pervades *every* aspect of our existence.

WE ARE "THE PILLAR AND SUPPORT OF THE TRUTH"

The example of truthfulness that Paul set may be inspiring, but is it really meant to be the standard for the rest of us? Certainly, apostles, preachers, and other Christian leaders must lead lives marked by complete honesty, but aren't ordinary Christians held to a less stringent standard? Not according to Scripture. There is no double standard when it comes to the truth.

Paul made this clear in his first letter to Timothy. He described "the church of the living God" as "the pillar and support of the truth" or, as worded in the *New International Version,* "the pillar and foundation of the truth" (3:15). What a startling statement! I would have expected to hear that God is the pillar of truth. But in 1 Timothy, Paul portrayed the church as the pillar that bears the truth.

The word *pillar* paints a powerful picture. Paul used a word that appears in the Greek Old Testament in the stirring story of Samson's final victory over the Philistines. Blind, defeated, and stripped of his supernatural power, Samson was dragged before the Philistine leaders so they could gloat over him as they offered sacrifices to their god. Leaning upon the two *pillars* that supported the house where they had gathered, Samson asked the Lord for one more burst of supernatural energy. God answered his prayer and Samson pushed the pillars over. The house fell upon all of the Philistines, who perished along with Samson.

The church supports the truth just as those pillars supported the Philistine house. If the church loses its strength, then truth will begin to topple. It will not tumble to the ground forever, but it will lose its impact upon the world for a while.

The strength of the church lies not only in its leaders but also in the people of God banded together. Scripture teaches that the church will fulfill its earthly calling only "as each part does its own special work" (Ephesians 4:16). None of us can say we are incidental to the church. If Christian leaders are truthful but ordinary Christians are not, then the church will not be strong enough to bear the weight of truth. Of course, if the leaders of the church fail to live truthfully, then the church will sustain great damage, and its truth-bearing work will be severely compromised. The case of the Roman Catholic Church's lack of candor over priestly scandals offers a tragic example. Only when all members of the church—both clergy and laity, both leaders and followers—seek to live in truth will the church fulfill its role as "the pillar and support of the truth."

What kind of truth are we to support? In Paul's correspondence with Timothy, truth is, first of all, the good news of God's work in Jesus Christ, the gospel that leads to our salvation. One of our primary tasks is to proclaim and preserve the truth of the gospel. Yet, as representatives of the truthful God, we are to support truth in all dimensions of life: in family and in friendship, at work and at play, in politics and in school. Wherever you are, you have the opportunity and calling to seek and to speak the truth.

My wife, Linda, has been a pillar of truth in our local school district. Owing to financial shortfalls, the district has faced an array of painful choices. One of these choices included the closing of our local elementary school. Because she had been so involved in the school, Linda was distressed not only about the possibility of its closing but also about the obscure communication coming from the school district. Administrators and school board members seemed unwilling to tell the public what was really going on. So, rather than simply get angry, Linda got going. She called district officials and e-mailed school board members. Unlike many parents from our school who sought to harass the district into keeping the school open, Linda sought the truth. What financial challenges was the district facing? What were the potential savings associated with closing our school? Were there other options? Linda soon earned the respect of school district leaders because of her frankness and commitment to the truth. She helped bring clarity in place of obscurity, candor in place of spin. So impressed were district administrators that they appointed Linda to a commission that is studying the costs and benefits of future school closures.

Linda's example illustrates a vital aspect of our calling as "the pillar and support of the truth." We are not merely to guard the truth by protecting it within the walls of the church, much as medieval monks protected biblical manuscripts from the battles that raged outside their monasteries. Rather, we are to be truthful people in the world. As Jesus said in the Sermon on the Mount, we are to let our light shine in the world, not hide it under a basket.[5] Even as the Father sent Jesus into the world with the truth, so Jesus has sent us.[6]

TRUTHFULNESS TESTED

Much of the time it's easy to shine with the light of truth. Ask me about the weather, and I'll tell you the truth. Ask me what's going on with the Lakers, and I'll gladly tell you the name of their top draft pick and where they stand within their division, especially when they're winning. No spin needed here, no temptation to lie. But I often face circumstances that test my commitment to truthfulness, and so do you. I am not referring only to occasions when we're tempted to lie. Often the more difficult challenges come when we're tempted simply to be less than fully truthful, when we can conveniently leave some things out while avoiding a lie in a technical sense. I encounter these trials all the time as friend, boss, taxpayer, professor, pastor, husband, and father.

Last night at dinner, for instance, Linda innocently asked me how I liked a birthday present I had recently received. As she and my children waited for my answer, I struggled with what to say. In truth I didn't really like the present—a dreadfully ugly shirt—at all. But it came from a relative who is a particular favorite of my children. If I told the truth in their presence, they would take it personally and feel hurt. Moreover, odds are good that they would tell the relative. I was tempted to shade the truth by saying something like "It's the best shirt I got this year." (Of course, it was the *only* shirt I'd received!) But in the end I told the truth without misleading anyone. "I don't know exactly what to say," I admitted, "but I do know that I am thankful for Lisa's generosity." Spinning—or even outright lying—would have been so much more comfortable.

We pastors have an especially difficult time being truthful. Just ask us about the attendance at our churches. We don't usually tell barefaced lies, but we do tend to round off numbers for the sake of our egos. A church of 260 members is "about 300." Anything over 800 can be rounded off nicely to "about 1,000." This practice is so common, in fact, that an unfortunate phrase has been coined: When pastors exaggerate the reach of their ministries, they are said to "speak evangelistically." Now that's a spin-drenched euphemism if I ever heard one!

Spin often rears its ugly head when churches are struggling. If our membership numbers are languishing, here comes the spin: "We've lost a few members recently, but they were the uncommitted folk anyway. We're actually a much stronger church now than we were before, unlike those churches that are growing too fast for their own good." Of course, this *may* be true, but I wonder. Don't you?

I know the temptation to exaggerate the size of my own congregation. Though my head knows better, my heart is still tempted to measure my worth as a pastor by the number of warm bodies in the pews. A few weeks ago I was talking with four other pastors about our personal and professional challenges. The conversation was progressing well, I thought, until one of the pastors asked how large my church was. I felt a strong desire to exaggerate because my church was *less than one-tenth* the average of their churches. My congregation includes about 750 adult members. The *average* church size of the other four pastors ran about 8,000. No lie. If I told the truth, the others might think less of me. So for a fleeting moment I considered adding youth and children to my membership number, which would at least have allowed me to say the word *thousand*. But I knew I'd be misrepresenting my ministry, so I told the truth. (I don't think it made a whit of difference to the other pastors, by the way. They seemed less impressed with the sizes of their churches than I was.)

Even if you're not a pastor, you still have similar struggles. Maybe you're tempted to exaggerate when the doctor asks, "So, how often do you exercise?" Or maybe your trial comes when a friend asks, "How are your kids?" two days after your teenager came home from a party with alcohol on her breath. I've watched men exaggerate their professional or athletic accomplishments. And I've seen women say just about anything to avoid hurting each other's feelings.

The challenge of fully honest living is magnified by the culture in which we live. Our society has a high tolerance for deception. Telling the truth, not to mention *living* it, is seen as moral extra credit, if it gets any credit at all. Sometimes it even flies in the face of a group's accepted values. Recently I overheard a conversation that illustrates this point. It seems that a student had given drugs to another student. When the recipient was caught with the drugs, the police asked him where he got them. He told the truth. Soon the student who had supplied the drugs was expelled from school. The parents whom I heard discussing this were friends with the expelled student's parents. They were highly critical of the young man who told the truth to the police. "He should have known enough to lie," one parent said. "He could have said he just found the drugs," another suggested. For this group of parents, loyalty to a friend meant much more than truthfulness.

Similarly, a man from my church shared with me his struggle to be truthful on the job. "Where I work, it's common, even expected," he said, "for people to lie in order to cover up their mistakes, the mistakes made by a coworker, and especially the boss's mistakes. If I were to be fully truthful, I'd soon be on the outs. I might even lose my job." This man's situation is similar to that of millions of Christians who want to be truthful, but who also worry that truthfulness might threaten their ability to provide for their families. I don't mean to minimize their struggle or suggest that there are easy answers. But I do know that God's call to truthfulness doesn't stop at the office door and that habitual deception poisons our spirits. If you find yourself in a job that demands dishonesty, I'd urge you to start asking the Lord for a new work situation. No matter what your salary, the personal price you're paying is too high.

If you're not convinced that truthfulness is a tough challenge, pay close attention to your conversations during the next week. You might be surprised by how many times you're tempted to be less than truthful—and by how many times you give way to that temptation, often without even recognizing it.

THE UNEXPECTED ATTRACTION OF TRUTH

Being truthful is a grand challenge, but it also presents a grand opportunity. Increasingly, people are longing for something to believe in, for someone they can trust. They are losing their tolerance for spin and are searching for straight talk. For example, during the last round of the 2000 presidential primaries, an article in the *Christian Science Monitor* proclaimed, "In Age of Spin, Voters Yearn for the Blunt."[7] The article examined the surprising popularity of Senator John McCain, attributing his success not so much to his views on issues as to his unusual honesty.

More and more, people are decrying the twisting of truth. A college student at the University of Illinois asked, "Has the truth become irrelevant?" in his column "No More Truth, Just Spin."[8] Another youthful critic complained, "Young people tend to be even more idealistic and are more reluctant to engage in an imperfect political system. We are sick of spin and image and being talked down to. No one wants to be suckered."[9] From Britain we hear the refrains, "We are becoming sick and tired of spin" and "Spin. Spin. I am sick of it."[10] On the other side of the globe, a New Zealander lamented, "Aren't YOU tired of spin-doctors.... DOWN WITH SPIN!!!!!"[11]

If there is indeed a growing intolerance of spin, then Christians have a stunning opportunity. If we respond to God's call to truthful living, not only will God be honored, not only will we live in the freedom of truth, but we also will find that people are drawn to our truthfulness and, more important, to the One who is the truth.

Honesty breaks down barriers to faith and opens people to hearing the gospel. Several years ago a woman came to me to "check out" Christianity. She brought a long list of tough questions, including some of the classics such as "Why does a good God allow suffering?" I tried to answer her questions, but I often bumped up against the limits of my understanding. I kept admitting my ignorance, saying things like, "You know, I'm not really sure I can answer that question adequately." After several of these admissions, the woman blurted out, "You keep on telling me that you don't have the answers I'm seeking." As I scrambled to apologize, she interrupted me: "No, I'm *not* upset with you. I'm relieved, actually. I've always thought Christians pretended to have all the answers. Your honesty about what you don't know makes me *more* inclined to believe you."

Ironically, the less truthful the world around us becomes, the more our truthfulness will stand out. Consider the tragic failure of Enron, the former energy giant that was propped up for years by misleading financial reports. The leaders of this multibillion dollar corporation spun a tangled web of falsehoods. Even their accounting firm became ensnared in the sticky deception. Not to anyone's surprise, when testifying before Congress, Enron executives tried desperately to spin themselves out of culpability. It's amazing what highly successful people can "forget" when it serves their purposes.

But in the midst of all of this mess, one Enron executive stood out from the rest. Sherron Watkins, a vice president, became unexpectedly famous for her attempt to tell the truth. Hoping to help avert financial disaster, she wrote a memo to Enron's chairman, Kenneth Lay. In the memo Ms. Watkins complained about many of the company's financial deceptions. She wrote, "I am incredibly nervous that we will implode in a wave of accounting scandals. My eight years of Enron work history will be worth nothing on my résumé, the business world will consider the past successes as nothing but an elaborate accounting hoax."[12] Sherron was aware that writing this memo might lead to her being fired, but she felt compelled to speak the truth even at great risk.

What in the world drove Sherron Watkins to stand out from the crowd? The simple answer is her Christian commitment. She grew up in a Christian family and continues to be an active member of the First Presbyterian Church of Houston. There she has been regularly involved in an adult Sunday-school class known as the B.A.S.I.C. class—Brothers and Sisters in Christ. When members of the news media decided to find out what made Sherron such an exemplary truth teller, they questioned the teacher of her Sunday-school class. He explained, "Sherron is probably the most amazed person in the world that this has stirred up front-page headlines all over the world. *She just believes that she is called to live the truth.*"[13] She dared to be true, no matter what the consequences.

Sadly, Sherron Watkins's truthfulness didn't stave off the corporate implosion that she feared. Truth telling doesn't always lead to a happy ending this side of heaven. But Sherron did what she knew to be right. And, as it turned out, she drew positive attention not just to herself, but to the truthful Lord whom she serves. Even the usually skeptical press wrote glowingly about her distinctive commitment to truth. In fact, *Time* magazine recognized her as one of three "Persons of the Year" for 2002.[14]

THE WEIGHTINESS OF TRUTH

My conviction that truthfulness can make a pronounced difference in our world doesn't depend merely on the growing dislike of spin or the inspiring stories of people such as Sherron Watkins. It is based on the very nature of truth. There is power in the truth, a power that dwarfs the superficial strength of spin. Truth has power to reveal, to enlighten, to transform, to vanquish evil, and to endure. As Aleksandr Solzhenitsyn said in his acceptance speech upon winning the Nobel Prize for Literature, "One word of truth outweighs the whole world."[15] In 1970, with the Soviet Union at the height of its fearsome power, Solzhenitsyn's confidence in truth seemed hopelessly idealistic. But two decades later, as the Berlin Wall tumbled and, along with it, the Soviet attempt to twist the truth in the interests of communism, the Russian novelist was proved right. One word of truth does indeed outweigh the whole world.

Yet the power of truth is not self-generated. Truth draws its dynamism from its inseparable connection with the God of truth. Similarly, our truthfulness will come not simply from our personal desire for freedom or from the worthy goal of drawing people to Christ, but from our inseparable connection with the Truthful Trinity. The more we draw near to God, the more we will fulfill his calling to live truthfully.

Yet this calling isn't an easy one. It involves risk. It requires that we reject the comfortable and familiar ways of our world. In order to be truthful people, we must first reject falsehood. It is to this challenge that we turn in chapter 3.

SPURNING SPIN

THE REJECTION THAT REFRESHES

L ike most Americans, I grew up inspired by the legendary honesty of George Washington. As a young boy I learned that when he chopped down his father's prized cherry tree, he freely admitted his misdemeanor. Along with millions of American children, I was encouraged to be truthful just like young George.

The history of the cherry tree story is itself a remarkable tale. It first appeared in the writings of an ordained minister, Mason Locke Weems. Parson Weems attempted parish ministry in the late eighteenth century, but without success. So he turned to writing and selling self-improvement books. In the early nineteenth century, Weems traveled throughout the eastern United States, hawking his spiritually uplifting wares to thousands of Americans who sought to be improved.

One of his masterpieces was called *A History of the Life and Death, Virtues and Exploits of General George Washington.* In this book of moral lessons, Weems penned the famous story of six-year-old George, who chopped down his father's cherry tree. Then he was confronted by his father who asked, "George, do you know who killed that beautiful little cherry tree yonder in the garden?" Allow Parson Weems to finish this story in his own inimitable words:

This was a tough question; and George staggered under it for a moment; but quickly recovered himself: and looking at his father,

with the sweet face of youth brightened with the inexpressible charm
of all-conquering truth, he bravely cried out: "I can't tell a lie, Pa; you
know I can't tell a lie. I did cut it with my hatchet." "Run to my arms,
you dearest boy," cried his father in transports, "run to my arms; glad
am I, George, that you killed my tree; for you have paid me for it a
thousand fold. Such an act of heroism in my son is more worth than a
thousand trees, though blossomed with silver, and their fruits of purest
gold."[1]

What a stirring climax to this story, poignantly narrated by a minister seeking
to commend truthfulness to Americans.

I'm sad to say, however, that there's no evidence this event ever occurred.
Nothing in Washington's memoirs or his family history suggests that he ever
felled the tree or confessed to his father. Weems, it appears, felt the freedom to
invent edifying stories to advance his moral agenda, not to mention his own
financial well-being. His book on Washington is filled with many other histor-
ically dubious but inspirational episodes, in addition to the celebrated cherry
tree tale.

Ironically, Weems's book illustrates how deeply deception is embedded in
American culture, not to mention in the human soul. In the spirit of can-do
pragmatism, we all too easily rationalize a fiction that is passed off as truth.
Hence, Parson Weems told outright lies to bolster the moral character of his
readers.

Lying is so common in today's media-saturated world that we may be
tempted to yearn for the mythical good ol' days when everyone was honest. But
that utopia never existed. Though modern media have broadcast the seeds of
deception, its roots burrow deeply into every human heart. Thus, if we are
going to be fully truthful people, we must identify the weeds of falsehood both
in our private gardens and in the common garden of public life, and then we
must intentionally yank them out. If we are to be completely honest, both in
speech and in heart, we must spurn spin.

SPEAK THE TRUTH, REJECT FALSEHOOD

The apostle Paul dealt with spin as wisely as anyone. As he confronted the deceptive practices of his religious and philosophical competitors, he did two essential things: He spoke the truth and he rejected falsehood. If that sounds redundant, take a closer look.

To the Corinthians, Paul wrote, "We reject all shameful and underhanded methods. We do not try to trick anyone, and we do not distort the word of God. We tell the truth before God, and all who are honest know that" (2 Corinthians 4:2). He went out of his way to repudiate the secrecy, trickery, and verbal sleight of hand so common among his rivals. He chose not only to speak truth but also to reject deception in all forms.

Such a two-edged commitment to truthfulness is required of all Christians. In Ephesians 4 Paul encourages us to reject falsehood even as we embrace truth: "[When we become mature in Christ,] we will no longer be like children, forever changing our minds about what we believe because someone has told us something different or because someone has cleverly lied to us and made the lie sound like the truth. Instead, we will hold to the truth in love." (verses 14-15). Paul does more than urge us to "hold to the truth." He also urges us to avoid the trickery, craftiness, and deceit that batter our truthfulness—to translate his Greek words more literally. On the one hand, we must be on guard so that we will not be hoodwinked by such things. On the other hand, we must watch ourselves to ensure that we do not employ the same practices in our own lives.

If it's true that we can't fully speak the truth unless we first reject falsehood, what are we to do with this insight? The answer is: If our goal is to be truthful people, we can't simply add truth to our repertoire. We must also root out deception, even when we can be deceptive without actually lying—the field in which most spin doctors have earned their Ph.D.'s.

Spurning spin may be difficult, but it doesn't require complex strategies. Basically, it involves three simple steps.

1. *Make a commitment to avoid deception.* If you intend to "put away all

falsehood" (Ephesians 4:25), don't think it will happen just by wishful thinking. You need to make a conscious commitment to consistent, comprehensive truth-full-ness in all of life. "Trying" not to lie won't do it. Without a willful commitment to avoid deception, you'll never be able to resist and reject the corrosive influence of spin, and you will be a ready victim for the rationalizations that seem so attractive when you're tempted to be less than fully honest.

A woman in my church, who took my preaching on truthfulness to heart, dedicated herself to speaking the truth in all her daily interactions. Sure enough, she soon found herself tempted to lie. She wanted to compliment her friend's haircut even though she didn't like it. She also really wanted to avoid telling her husband how much she had spent on a new decoration for their living room. But because she had made a commitment to herself and to the Lord, she took the risky and unfamiliar path of honesty. In the end she experienced the peace that comes from daring to be true.

Let me urge you to share your commitment to rejecting deceit with people who can support you and hold you accountable. And, of even greater importance, ask God for his help. Since deception is often known only to God and to the deceiver, your accountability partners won't always be able to call your bluff. But God can. You will be able to banish spin only by his grace—grace that is freely available through the Holy Spirit.

2. *Learn how to recognize deception.* This isn't as easy as it sounds. Deception, by definition, is deceptive. It hides. It fools us. It is difficult to recognize, even in ourselves. In the study conducted by Professor Robert Feldman, the students whose conversations were videotaped were shocked when they realized they had been lying in casual conversation. The reason for their shock? It's easy to lie to ourselves about being liars. In Feldman's experiment, the students never questioned their own truthfulness until they watched themselves on video.[2]

Most of us won't be in a position to observe on videotape the way we interact with others. But if we have made a commitment to avoid falsehood, then we'll be much more aware of the ways in which we dabble in deception. Moreover, if we seek God's help, the Holy Spirit will clearly show us our deception.

As you begin to analyze your communication patterns, you'll discover a number of predictable settings in which you are tempted to bend or break the truth. (I'll address some of the most common contexts later in this chapter.) Deception often occurs when we attempt to get out of trouble, promote something we believe in (especially ourselves), or manage the feelings of others.

3. *Actively reject deception.* Once we have identified deception, we must take the necessary step of rejecting it. Of course, this can be hard, even excruciating, especially if we're not accustomed to truthfulness. Even relatively petty lies, if they are habitual, can challenge our will. If, for instance, you tend to voice agreement with the opinions of others on politics or even about a movie because you want to avoid conflict, you will find it tough to overcome this practice. Your commitment to reject deception must be stronger than your fear of disagreeing and risking the loss of another's approval or friendship.

In light of this difficulty, it becomes clear why we need Scripture on our side. Paul's simple phrasing in Ephesians 4:25, "Put away all falsehood," shapes our behavior like the exhortation of a Little League coach who urges, "Don't take your eyes off the ball!" Of course, Paul's counsel in Ephesians echoes the ninth commandment: "Thou shalt not bear false witness against thy neighbour" (Exodus 20:16, KJV). This commandment, like most of the other nine, comes in the form of a prohibition—"Thou shalt not"—rather than a positive command— "Thou shalt." God knows our natural tendency to shade the truth, so he states the command as a ban against falsehood. The starkness of "Thou shalt not bear false witness" penetrates beneath the armor of our rationalizations. Like the videotaped conversations in Feldman's experiment, the prohibition against falsehood opens our eyes to our habitual reliance on spin.[3]

But must we really swear off *all* deception? Is it wrong, for example, to pretend to be a horse as you carry your toddler on your back? What about making up stories to entertain friends or to illustrate a point as you teach others? It depends. Pretending is an essential and morally acceptable part of imaginative play as long as all parties understand the rules of the game. If your toddler knows you're not *really* a horse, there is no deception involved. If, however, you claim to be a monster while playing with a child who doesn't realize that you're just pretending, then your deception is hurtful. (Yes, I have done this, I'm embarrassed to admit.) Similarly, it's fine to make up stories. Jesus did so in his most memorable parables. But, once again, the storyteller must clarify the fictional character of the narrative for the listeners.

We live in a world that constantly blurs the lines between fiction and non-fiction. Ronald Reagan's official biographer inserted an imaginary character into a supposedly historical biography and defended his effort as consistent with his creative license.[4] Then, a Pulitzer Prize-winning historian and professor made up stories of his combat experience in Vietnam in order to enliven his college lectures. In defense of the professor, the Reagan biographer wrote in the *New York Times,* "Well, of course he's woven the fabric of his life partly out of whole cloth and partly out of the shot silk of fantasy.... Can any of us gaze into the bathroom mirror and whisper, 'I never made anything up'?"[5]

Given our world's growing tolerance of deception, Christians must reject even the appearance of falsehood. The only acceptable use of fiction in conversation is when all hearers understand that we are playing a game and they know the rules. A preacher I know told a funny story in a sermon, pretending it had happened to a few members of his church. After the service several people commented on the story as if it were true. When the preacher explained that the anecdote was fictitious, these people felt as if they had been deceived. It would serve this preacher well in the future to be more careful about confusing truth and fiction, even when he's just having fun.

In my own preaching I make every effort to avoid this confusion. At times I will change names or incidental particulars of a story in order to protect a person's privacy. My congregation knows this because I tell them so every now and then. Yet they trust that I don't alter the essence of a story or exaggerate details to liven things up. (By the way, in case you didn't read the notice on the copyright page of this book, you should be aware that I follow the same practice in writing as in preaching.)

WHERE DECEPTION LURKS

Even if you're constantly vigilant in guarding against falsehood, chances are still good that you're not completely free of deception. I confess that I've been caught in this web, as you'll soon see.

To help us identify the deceptions we're often blind to, let's examine three contexts in which we may be tempted to deceive. These life settings test our commitment to spurning spin. They've certainly tested mine!

Context One: Perjured Promotion

The context of promotion and publicity frequently tempts us to exaggerate. Of course, it's easy to accuse Madison Avenue while excusing ourselves. Sure, the pros engage in plenty of spin in their efforts to sell candy and candidates, but so do we in promoting ourselves or our pet causes.

Have you read any résumés recently? Incidental assignments grow into major responsibilities. Modest accomplishments become unparalleled triumphs. The recent case of George O'Leary provides a prominent and sad example. He landed a dream job as head football coach at Notre Dame only to resign five days later. Why did he quit? Because it was discovered that he had lied about his academic and athletic accomplishments on his résumé. Though he was an outstanding coach, his deceptions overwhelmed his legitimate qualifications for the job. O'Leary was forced to give up his dream.

But he's not alone. I recently came across a dossier of a person I know. As I read it, I was impressed by how she could make even dismal failures sound like noteworthy achievements. If you've had to apply for a job recently, you know how tempting it is to portray your accomplishments as far bigger than life to make your application stand out above the competition.[6] The legitimate task of making yourself look attractive to a prospective employer does not excuse exaggeration or fabrication. As we write a résumé, we need to ask ourselves continually, "Did I *really* accomplish these things? Am I misleading anyone who might use this résumé to make a hiring decision?"

If you've ever been involved in sales or marketing, you've no doubt experienced the temptation to mislead. When I was in graduate school, I managed a center that offered tutoring to students who were preparing to take standardized exams. Part of my job was to generate publicity for our program. The best promotion of all was to boast about the improved test scores achieved by our clients. We could, indeed, demonstrate such improvement. But I still faced a delicate communication challenge. Most of the students in our test-preparation course showed a significant gain on the SAT—an average gain of 120 points among those whose scores improved. However, a few students actually received *lower* scores!

If my promotional material spoke only of the average improvement, rather than the average overall change, I could eliminate the scores of the students who didn't improve. How easy it was to state the literal truth—"the average improvement after taking our class is 120 points"—in a way that led people to believe that the average student increased his or her score by that margin. In truth, however, the average student improved by only 90 points, if I took into account those who registered a lower score after completing our program.

I faced a dilemma. If I spoke of average *improvement,* I wasn't lying, technically speaking. I was, however, putting a deceptive spin on the truth. So what did I, the future writer of a book on truthfulness, do? I spun like the best of them. Our promotional literature escaped an outright lie, but it didn't tell the complete truth. I'm sad to say that in this instance I failed to renounce the trickery of this world.

Temptations like these confront us all the time. I know of one outstanding Christian ministry that claimed to have brought significant church renewal to one-quarter of the churches in my own denomination. I wish that were true! But it isn't. A truth-seeking friend of mine tracked down the source of the figure used in the organization's promotional literature. He found that it was based on a survey of less than one percent of Presbyterian churches. In this survey, one-quarter of the congregations mentioned *using* this particular ministry. But that's as far as it went. There was no indication of whether exposure to the ministry had actually produced a positive change in those congregations. My friend alerted the national board of the ministry, which I hope has stopped using the groundless statistic in its publicity.

If we are going to live truthfully, then we need to renounce perjured promotion when we're trying to sell a product, a ministry, or even ourselves.

Context Two: Avoiding Accountability

In the last chapter we considered the story behind the collapse of the energy giant Enron and the continuing saga of leaders who avoid taking responsibility for their errors. How tempting it is for top executives to blame others or plead ignorance or do anything but confess culpability. When we see the stock market drop and fear that our retirement savings are shrinking to nothing, it's easy to get angry at greedy and blame-avoiding corporate executives. But you know what? I'm not all that different from them, and maybe you aren't either.

Just last week my willingness to admit my own failures was sorely tested. It happened when a subordinate mentioned in a staff meeting something that bothered him about our church. I'm not sure he realized that the incident he was criticizing was my fault. Frankly, I'm not sure I did either when the conversation began. But soon I could see that the buck was about to stop in front of me, and I didn't like it. I reacted defensively.

As the discussion continued and I was no longer able to duck responsibility for my mistake, I said, "Well, *perhaps* I *probably* should have done things differently." But then I stopped myself. There was no "perhaps" or "probably" about it. I was simply spinning myself out of accepting responsibility. I could try to place the blame elsewhere, just as the Enron execs had done, or I could renounce the ways of the world and fess up to my failure. By God's grace—and because of my work on this pesky book—I revised my statement: "I *definitely* should have acted differently, and I'm sorry that I didn't."

To be honest, I didn't like being confronted. Neither did I like my knee-jerk tendency to spin the truth. And I didn't like having to admit to the truth. But if I learn to be truthful in a group of eight brothers and sisters in Christ, hopefully I won't have to learn it in front of the whole country someday.

We live in a society of self-proclaimed victims. When politicians fail, they blame the economy, the smear campaign of the opposition, or the bias of the news media. Criminals blame a difficult childhood. Golfers blame fast greens. Professional basketball players are victims of bad refereeing. Child abusers are really just victims of those who abused them years earlier. And so it goes. A commitment to reject the spin of victimization and take responsibility for one's own life will not be easy to fulfill when our culture pushes us in the opposite direction.

I am not denying that there are real victims in our world, people worthy of compassion and patience. But I'm distressed over how readily people use the excuse of victimization to avoid accountability. Moreover, their claims of being victims of relatively trivial injuries make a mockery of genuine victimization. But even people who are genuine victims of terrible tragedies still must take responsibility for their own behavior.[7]

Context Three: Traffic and Tardiness

When is the last time someone showed up late for a meeting and said, "I'm sorry I'm late. I made some poor choices today and didn't plan my time well. It's entirely my fault that I've kept you waiting"? I'm tired of hearing about traffic. Everyone knows how much traffic there is at rush hour. Puh-leeeze!

I do understand the temptation to give the truth a few good spins when arriving late to a meeting, though. Just last Tuesday I showed up late for a church prayer meeting that I usually lead. I was so late, in fact, that I skipped the prayer meeting and instead went to a different room where the elder board would be gathering after the prayer session.

I had what I considered to be a good reason for missing the prayer meeting. The cause of my lateness, however, was a bit complicated. I didn't want to take up valuable board meeting time making excuses for my truancy. On the other hand, a simple statement of what I'd done would have put me in a bad light. I was sorely tempted to spin matters a bit: "I'm sorry I'm late. A *pastoral situation* came up and I was needed." Another option was: "I'm sorry I'm late. I was involved in a *family commitment* and needed to stick around." Neither of those explanations was a lie. Both of them sounded a whole lot better than the complete truth, which ran something like this: "I'm sorry I'm late. I was at a birthday party for my daughter's friend and really felt like it would be best for me to stay there and miss the prayer meeting." This birthday party was the "pastoral situation" as well as the "family commitment." But it would have been misleading to use either of these phrases in my excuse. So I admitted the truth and took a fair amount of ribbing for skipping prayer to party with a bunch of little girls. I deserved what I got, yet I still couldn't help thinking that "pastoral situation" would have provided a much more dignified excuse.

Why was I tempted to bend the truth to my advantage? I wanted to avoid embarrassment, and I wanted the elders to respect my judgment. In the short run, being completely honest wasn't much fun. But I felt good about my choice to be truthful. And, even though some of the elders might have questioned my judgment and most of them gave me a hard time, I think their trust in me actually increased because of my embarrassing honesty.

THE MAGNETISM OF FRANKNESS

If we intentionally spurn spin when we're promoting ourselves, when we're tested by accountability, and when we're tempted to make excuses for our behavior, we will often find ourselves in conflict with the world around us. In some cases we'll experience criticism, perhaps even ostracism, for our commitment to avoid deceit. The truth is that some people would prefer that we *not* tell them the full truth! Our culture values the ease and convenience of the well-chosen half-truth. On the other hand, there will be times when our courage to reject spin will attract people like moths to a porch light. Despite a pandemic of spin, deep inside people are hungering for honest, reliable, no-frills truth.

A couple of weeks after I preached a sermon on spurning spin, a parishioner named Steve told me about something that happened in a meeting at work. Prior to the meeting he had promised himself and God that he would no longer place blame elsewhere to excuse his own behavior. For instance, he vowed that if he showed up late for an appointment, he'd be completely honest about the reason. Sure enough, a few days later Steve failed to allow enough driving time to make it to a meeting.

Arriving a full twenty minutes after the meeting began, he took his seat and then apologized. "I'm sorry I'm late," he began. "Please forgive me. I can't blame anything for my lateness other than my own poor choices. I didn't allow enough time to get here. I'm truly sorry."

His honesty stunned everyone in the room. They didn't know how to respond. Finally, the leader of the meeting said, "Well, I'm sorry you're late too, but thanks for being honest about why. That's the kind of openness we need in this meeting."

All of a sudden the participants began talking about the benefits of greater honesty in their business. A few minutes into this lively conversation another person entered the room out of breath. He was even later than Steve, and he offered the usual "blame everything else" kind of excuse. The others in the room laughed because this man's spin looked foolish in light of Steve's gutsy honesty.

Steve said that throughout the rest of the day the quality of conversation in the meeting was unusually frank. That same tone continued in the days that followed. Steve's renunciation of spin was contagious and transformed the work environment.

Too often our desire to save face, avoid consequences, or prop up our sagging ego steers us away from telling the truth and robs us of the blessings of truth. Living in truth brings freedom and refreshment. After getting over their initial surprise, Steve's colleagues were energized by his candor. And they all benefited from the freedom of speaking more openly about their professional challenges. When Jesus said the truth would set us free, he wasn't speaking figuratively. The truth is renewing and liberating; it conveys tangible, practical benefits in daily life. It's sad that we deny ourselves these blessings by giving in to spin and deception.

Having said that, I realize that telling the hard truth will not always bring the immediate positive outcome Steve experienced. I know a woman who lost her job because she was unwilling to lie. Her boss demanded that she misrepresent her division's sales statistics to impress upper management. When she refused to follow her boss's orders, she was terminated. But even considering the risks that are associated with truth telling, Steve's story makes me wonder what might happen if we who are called to truthfulness simply started speaking the plain truth in all instances. How many friends, colleagues, employers, family members, neighborhoods, and churches would be transformed by the refreshing, liberating power of hearing the truth?

LINCOLN'S LONG WALK

Since I began this chapter by debunking the beloved story of George Washington and the cherry tree, let me end by mentioning another favorite account from American moral history—the long walk of Abraham Lincoln. You know the story. Young Lincoln was working in Mr. Offut's general store in New Salem, Illinois, when he accidentally overcharged a customer. By the time Lincoln discovered his error, the customer had gone home. Because her home was several miles away and because the overcharge was only a few cents, one would have expected Lincoln to forget about it, or at least to wait until the woman next visited the store. But "Honest Abe" knew he had to refund the money owed the woman, and, without delay, he walked the miles required to return the pennies.

Unlike the case of George and the tree, historical evidence confirms this account of Lincoln and his long walk.[8] Why has this story been told again and again in the last two centuries? Because it teaches a vital lesson and it's also so *unusual*. Most of us would not go to such great lengths for the sake of a few cents, even if our personal integrity were at stake. We'd go along with conventional wisdom: "There's no harm done. After all, it's just a couple of pennies." But Abraham Lincoln rejected the societal norm. Honesty was worth the long walk.

Though the story of Abraham Lincoln, the honest shop clerk, is memorable, the less familiar story of Abraham Lincoln, the honest shop owner, is even more impressive. While living in New Salem, Lincoln and a partner bought a general store and attempted to run it as a profitable business. But owing to unwise investments and general mismanagement, the store finally "winked out," to use Lincoln's own phrase. Not long thereafter his partner died, leaving the unfortunate Lincoln with what he called the "National Debt." But unlike many others who went bankrupt in frontier ventures and skipped town to escape their creditors, Lincoln promised to repay every cent he owed. He fulfilled this promise even though it took him more than fifteen years to retire the debt. When Abraham Lincoln made a commitment, his word was good as gold. No matter what those around him were doing, his life and his words were filled with honesty.[9]

We mustn't simply stand back and marvel at Lincoln's integrity. We must step forward and imitate it. God's Word calls us to rise above the world's standard—to be different from the usual. A commitment to truthfulness requires that we reject conventional wisdom when that wisdom condones deception, even seemingly harmless deception. It calls us to spurn spin, since spin will always prevent us from speaking with complete honesty. Sometimes it will seem as if we're walking miles out of our way for a few cents worth of truthfulness, but in the end this effort will pay rich rewards.

FACING THE TRUTH
WE'D RATHER AVOID

CONFESSION AND THE NEW CREATION

My friends and I were crowded into the back of Bill Hurst's mother's station wagon on the way to a Cub Scout meeting. Seeking to impress my buddies, I gestured offensively out the back window—not even stopping to consider that my actions were reflected perfectly in the car's rearview mirror. I was caught in the act! And Mrs. Hurst, who witnessed the whole debacle, wasn't impressed by my boyish daring. Stopping the car, she ordered me to get out. She actually sent me home right on the spot.

As I walked the half-mile home, I was mortified at having been caught and terrified of facing my parents. I wasn't exactly sure what was wrong with that particular gesture, but I knew it was something I shouldn't have done.

When I got home, my mother noted that I was early. "Mark," she asked, "what happened to the scout meeting?"

I was in a jam, caught in the act all over again. So I did the first thing that came to mind. I lied.

"Mrs. Hurst sent me home early because she thought I made a nasty finger sign," I explained. "But she was wrong, Mom. It was one of the other guys who did it. I was just waving out the window."

A classic defense. When you get caught, blame the other guy. It's the oldest excuse in the book. It's also the oldest excuse in the Book.

ADAM POINTS THE FINGER

In the opening chapters of Genesis, God created the heavens and the earth and everything that fills them. He crowned this masterpiece with the creation of human beings. Placing them in a lush garden, God invited them to enjoy all the fruit that was growing there, with the exception of one tree. "You may freely eat any fruit in the garden," the Lord explained, "except fruit from the tree of the knowledge of good and evil. If you eat of its fruit, you will surely die" (2:16-17).

Then the crafty serpent stopped by and tempted the woman to taste the forbidden fruit. At first she resisted, explaining what God had said about eating and dying. "You won't die," the serpent ob-jected. "God knows that your eyes will be opened when you eat it. You will become just like God, knowing everything, both good and evil" (3:4-5). How clever the serpent was! If you compare what he said with the rest of the story, you'll notice that it was true… in a way.

Wait just a minute! Satan, the Father of Lies, speaking the truth? Technically, yes. After eating the fruit, the man and woman did not instantly die—*physically*. And they did become like God in the sense that they now knew the difference between good and evil, whereas before they knew only good. Here we find out that the serpent was the original spin doctor, using half-truths to deceive others into doing his bidding. And we thought spin was created by Madison Avenue!

The woman fell for the half-truth and ate the banned fruit, giving some to her husband. The first humans intentionally disobeyed, choosing to do what God had made clear was sin. They rejected God's benevolent guidance in favor of their own self-destructive autocracy.

The immediate result was the loss of openness in relationship. Seeing their nakedness in a sin-tinted light, the man and woman tried to cover themselves. Just as they hid parts of their bodies, they would soon hide their hearts as well. Step one was falling for a lie and disobeying God. Step two was hiding. Now brace yourself for step three: Spin is about to make its grand, grotesque entrance into human history.

When the man and woman heard God walking in the garden, they hid in the woods. The delightful openness with God that they formerly enjoyed had been lost. Yet God didn't take their evasive action as an answer. He knew they were hiding, but he still called out to them, "Where are you?" (3:9).

The man replied, "I heard you, so I hid. I was afraid because I was naked" (3:10). So far the man was truthful, but not for long.

God followed up with another question: "Who told you that you were naked?" Then, even more to the point, he inquired, "Have you eaten the fruit I commanded you not to eat?" (3:11).

The honest answer to God's question would have been a simple, straight-forward "yes." But Adam, now caught in the act, answered, "Yes…but it was the woman you gave me who brought me the fruit, and I ate it" (3:12). What a diabolically shrewd response! The man knew he couldn't deny the facts right to God's face, so he did the next best thing: He pointed the finger of blame else-where. Literally, he fingered the woman, but the form of his excuse actually put the blame on God. "The woman *you gave me,* she's to blame!" the man asserted. John Calvin commented:

> Yet, just as if conscious of no evil, he puts his wife as the guilty party in his place. "Therefore I have eaten," he says, "because she gave." And not content with this, he brings, at the same time, *an accusation against God;* objecting that the wife, who had brought ruin upon him, had been given by God.[1]

"Well now," the original man reasoned, "if God had wanted me to avoid the forbidden fruit, then he shouldn't have given me such a fallible and persuasive partner!" Adam claimed to be a victim of both his partner's folly and God's lack of foresight.

When God turned to the woman, she also tried to avoid taking any responsibility, blaming her eating on the serpent's trickery. At least she didn't have the audacity to suggest that it was God's fault because he created the serpent and then allowed it into the garden. Nevertheless, she joined her husband as a self-appointed victim.

Notice that the man and the woman did not lie to God. Like the serpent, they told the truth, after a fashion. The woman did indeed give the fruit to the hapless man, as he claimed. God did indeed give the woman to the man, as the man quickly reminded God. And the serpent did indeed trick the woman into eating, as she maintained. These were all true statements, but they sidestepped the *heart* of the truth, substituting excuse and blame for complete honesty. Neither human stated the core truth that needed to be expressed: "Yes, I did eat the fruit you commanded me not to eat, Lord. I disobeyed you. I sinned." This was the truth they sought to avoid because it was so painful to acknowledge.

YOU AND ME AND ADAM AND EVE

I can't read this story without seeing myself in it. Not only have I done what God has forbidden—plenty of times—but I also have imitated the pathetic attempts of the man and woman to explain away obvious sin. As a brash Cub Scout, I was just like the first humans when I tried to spin my way out of trouble—"Another kid raised his middle finger, Mom. I was just waving out the window." And I continue to be like Adam and Eve each time I employ partial truths to cover up my sin.

Can you relate to the first humans as I can? John Calvin thought you should. After nailing the man for his attempt to explain away his sin, Calvin added, "We also, trained in the same school of original sin, are too ready to resort to subterfuges of the same kind."[2] Some of us resort to Adam's wife-blaming ruse. "I don't want to divorce my wife," a man rationalized as he sought my pastoral approval, "but it's clear that *she* doesn't want to be married to me anymore, even though she pretends like she does. This divorce is really her fault, even if I'm the one who has to seek it." Maybe he had succeeded in convincing himself, but he wasn't fooling me.

Do you remember Geraldine, the popular character in the repertoire of the late comedian Flip Wilson? "She" popularized the expression "The devil made me do it." This, of course, echoes Eve's classic excuse in the garden. But today's champion excuse-makers are too sophisticated to lay blame at the feet of the serpent. We've greatly enlarged the cast of characters who must be to blame for our blunders. Our parents have wounded us, and we're just acting out our pain. The entertainment industry has corrupted us, and we're just imitating the scenes we see in movies and music videos. The government has shortchanged us, so it's okay to cheat on our taxes. Even the church has damaged us, so don't blame us for our unchristian actions.

Again, we're brought back to the matter of partial truths. The excuses just listed might begin with objective truth. Many people *have* been hurt, and they desperately need healing. Past hurts can produce a disposition toward certain attitudes and behaviors. But being wounded does not excuse sinful behavior. If we hide behind a wall of excuses and fail to take responsibility for our sin, we resemble the first man and woman, who holed up in the woods in an attempt to conceal their sinful selves from God. Not only is this silly when you consider God's omniscience, but it's also self-defeating because only God can forgive our sins and cleanse our hearts. Truthfully and humbly admitting we're wrong is the only course that brings freedom.

Dave's Folly—and Ours

One of my most frustrating experiences in ministry involved a man named Dave. He had sought out pastoral guidance because he believed God was punishing him unjustly.

"How is God punishing you?" I asked.

"Everything was going great in my life," he explained. "I had the perfect job and the perfect fiancée. But I lost it all. My fiancée dumped me, and I got fired from my job. I don't know why God is doing this to me."

"How could this have happened?" I wondered aloud. "It sounds terrible."

Dave's story, which began with the sad tale of falling victim to God's injustice, slowly circled around to the truth. He had been working in his perfect job, where he met the woman who became his perfect fiancée. One day at work he caught his intended flirting with another employee. The two admitted they'd been having "a little fling." So Dave slugged his fiancée in the face, right in front of witnesses. That very day she dumped him, and he lost his job. (How many companies would keep a man on the payroll after he assaulted a fellow employee?) When I suggested to Dave that perhaps God was not punishing him, but that he was experiencing the consequences of his own rash behavior, he failed to see the connection.

"I'm a good guy," he insisted. "I made a mistake, that's all. It was a moment of anger. Besides, I was feeling a lot of pressure at work that day. I couldn't help myself. I don't know why God is punishing me for making one mistake."

I tried again, sharing what Scripture teaches about our sin: "If we say we have no sin, we are only fooling ourselves and refusing to accept the truth" (1 John 1:8). But Dave was blinded by folly and untruth. After I met with him a couple more times, it became clear that he wasn't ready to take responsibility for his actions and ask God to forgive him. We can't confess our sins and seek forgiveness as long as we deny our need for forgiveness.

It's easy to see the folly of Dave's spin. But most of us are closer to Dave than we want to admit. We don't punch people with our fists, but we strike blows with our words. Or we punish others with our silence. Or we batter innocents with our gossip. Or we withhold forgiveness even after another person humbly confesses his or her wrongdoing. Yet no matter what the nature of our offense is, as long as we imagine ourselves to be innocent when we have sinned, we cut ourselves off from God's grace. If we're going to receive divine forgiveness, we must face the truth we'd rather avoid: the truth of our sinfulness, the truth of our rebellion against God.

FACING THE TRUTH OF OUR SIN

King David stands alone in Scripture with this description: a man after God's own heart (see 1 Samuel 13:14). As a teenager he was chosen by the Lord to become king of Israel. Yet he was also a sinner of the highest (or lowest) magnitude. We find a detailed description of one of his most grievous sins in 2 Samuel 11–12. After spying a beautiful woman while she was taking a bath, David used his royal power to seduce her even though she was married to one of David's most faithful soldiers. When Bathsheba later informed the king that she was pregnant, he tried to cover up his sin by recalling her husband, Uriah, from the battlefield and ordering him to sleep with his wife. When this plan failed, David had Uriah killed in battle. Then he married Bathsheba.

At first David avoided dealing with his sin, trying instead to conceal it. No doubt his devious plans for Uriah reflected the denial in his own heart. (Even kings ordained by God are not immune from deception.) But when conscience failed to bring David to account, God sent the prophet Nathan to confront him. Finally David admitted his sin to Nathan, to himself, and to the Lord.

The substance of David's confession to God is recorded in Psalm 51. There he prayed,

> For I recognize my shameful deeds—
>> they haunt me day and night.
> Against you, and you alone, have I sinned;
>> I have done what is evil in your sight.
> You will be proved right in what you say,
>> and your judgment against me is just. (verses 3-4)

To be sure, David wronged both Bathsheba and Uriah. But his sin was primarily against God because David rebelled against God and his will. When David finally rejected his earlier denial, he began to regard his actions not as unfortunate mistakes but as evil deeds worthy of divine judgment.

Even before we confess our sins, we must first see them for what they are. So often we try to convince ourselves that we aren't actually "sinners." We may commit slip-ups, gaffes, and oversights, but surely not sins or evil deeds. We would do well to learn from David's example of truth telling and call our sin *sin,* plain and simple.

CONFESSING OUR SINS

Even if we're not stuck in denial, sometimes we confess our errors so generally that we miss the benefits that result from true confession. A rushed "Forgive me, Lord" may reflect our desire to say the right words without honestly dealing with our behavior or the condition of our hearts. Several years ago I was guiding a group through various modes of prayer. When I got to confession, I encouraged folks to be specific with the Lord about where they had missed the mark. Almost immediately I was interrupted by a man who pulled the rug out from under our confession. "We thank you, Lord," he prayed with gusto, "that we're forgiven through Jesus Christ. We don't have to worry about our sin anymore. We don't have to dwell on the past. We can claim our forgiveness and move on." "Now, Pastor, let's move on in this prayer meeting!" he clearly meant.

This man's unwillingness to be specific in confession is a common failing that stands in direct opposition to the requirements of Scripture. Note carefully the words in a crucial passage from John's first letter: "If we confess our sins, he who is faithful and just will forgive us our sins and cleanse us from all unrighteousness" (1:9, NRSV). The Greek verb translated "confess" means "to state something emphatically," even when that something is our own wrongdoing. When we confess our sins, we state what we have done and agree that it was wrong. The verse from 1 John uses a verb form that commends *ongoing* confession. It's not something we do once and that's that; rather, it's something we continue to do throughout our lives. Furthermore, the plural noun, *sins,* reminds us to acknowledge not just the general fact that we are sinful, but our particular actions that have dishonored God.

Though I tend to admit my most obvious sins to God each day, periodically I also take a couple of hours for in-depth confession. I ask the Holy Spirit to reveal what I need to confess. Though I usually begin with "the regulars," in time I consider areas of sin that I typically overlook. Sometimes I see wrong attitudes or behaviors that I've never acknowledged. Detailed confession isn't pleasant, of course, but it's an essential aspect of confronting the truth about my life that I'd rather avoid. We need to speak the truth to God about our sins, just as we need to be truthful in all other areas of life.

Confession of sin also is a key component in helping us overcome deception so that we can live truthful lives. When examining our lives, many of us need to be specific in confessing our sins of deception. Some of these may be so common in our behavior and in our culture that we need the Spirit's help to recognize them as sin. But we also may be fully aware of our dishonesty and perhaps have even resolved not to perpetuate it, yet we have never confessed it. Choosing not to confess recognized sin is the same as saying we aren't yet fully committed to repenting of it. Jumping immediately into attempting to resolve sin neglects the biblical call to confess and keeps us from tapping into the very strength that helps us act on our resolve. Full disclosure in confessing sin is the truth that helps set us free from those sins.

The Main Reason for Confession

Why should we confess our sins? "Because the Bible says so" is a sufficient but incomplete reason. The Bible teaches us to confess in order to experience divine forgiveness and all that follows from it. But this points to a still deeper reason for confession.

The main reason we confess has to do with *who God is* and *what God has done*. In Psalm 51 David cried out, "Have mercy on me, O God, because of your unfailing love. Because of your great compassion, blot out the stain of my sins" (verse 1). He knew God to be the Lord who revealed himself to Israel as "the merciful and gracious God...slow to anger and rich in unfailing love and faithfulness" (Exodus 34:6). As Christians who know God through Jesus Christ, we read Psalm 51 with the unparalleled proof of God's mercy and grace. According to Romans 5, "God showed his *great love* for us by sending Christ to die for us while we were still sinners" (verse 8). Moreover, "by his *boundless mercy*" God has allowed us to be born again (1 Peter 1:3). Therefore, we confess our sins because of who God is and with utter confidence in what he will do in response, in keeping with his gracious and merciful nature.

Notice again what John wrote in his first letter: "If we confess our sins, he who is faithful and just will forgive us" (1:9, NRSV). We confess, in part, because God is *faithful*. If we were speaking biblical Hebrew, we would say that he is a God of *'emet*—faithfulness and truth. We believe God's promises of forgiveness because he speaks the truth. We trust these promises because he is forever faithful. And we confess our sins because of who God is: the God of *'emet*.

From the beginning of Genesis onward, the Bible reveals God as One who seeks relationship with us. He is the God who comes looking for his people, the Good Shepherd who seeks his lost sheep, the Father who runs to embrace his long-lost son. Through confession we make ourselves available to be found by God. It's not mere ritual or some empty religious obligation, but the act of a heart broken by sin, a heart yearning for God. To this heart God responds with gracious forgiveness, as David affirmed, "The sacrifice you want is a broken spirit. A broken and repentant heart, O God, you will not despise" (Psalm 51:17). We confess because we know that God will not reject our repentance but will embrace us in his love.

Thus the fundamental reason for our confession is God's own nature and the revelation of that nature through Christ. Even before we lay our sin before God, we are confident of the outcome. We know he loves us and will show us mercy. He will not despise our genuine confession but will accept it, offering forgiveness and cleansing in return.

THE BENEFITS OF CONFESSION

If God were not who he is, then confession would be useless. In fact, if we did not have confidence in God's grace, then admitting our sins to a holy, omnipotent, perfect Judge would be the scariest thing in life. But because God is a God of *'emet*, of truth and faithfulness, we know that confession begets rich benefits.

Benefit One: Confession Leads to Reconciliation with God

One of the most precious of these benefits is reconciliation with God. For example, David asked the following of God:

> Don't keep looking at my sins...
> Do not banish me from your presence,
>   and don't take your Holy Spirit from me....
> Forgive me for shedding blood. (Psalm 51:9,11,14)

Each of these requests rightly assumes that sin puts a barrier between us and God that we can't possibly remove. David ached for God to take down this barrier. He knew that only God can choose to turn his gaze away from our sin. Only God can forgive us by refusing to let what we have done break our relationship with him. Only God's mercy allows us to remain in his holy presence even though we are sinners.

As we observed earlier in this chapter, one of the first and most devastating results of human sin is a breach in our relationship with God. No sooner did the first man and woman disobey God than they skulked off into the woods to hide from him. Not long thereafter the Lord expelled them from paradise, the place of unbroken fellowship with him. Yet, in his mercy, God acted in Christ to reconcile us to himself. We experience this reconciliation once and for all when we put our trust in Christ as our Lord and Savior. Furthermore, God has given us confession so that we might experience the reconciliation we have with him and so that we might grow in our relationship with him even when we sin.

Benefit Two: Confession Leads to Inner Cleansing

A further benefit of confession is inner cleansing. Sin pollutes our hearts like industrial waste spewing into a trout stream. When we sense our soul's contamination, we long to be made clean. Hence we join David in praying,

> Blot out the stain of my sins.
> Wash me clean from my guilt.

Purify me from my sin....
Remove the stain of my guilt. (Psalm 51:1,2,9)

Have you ever prayed like this? As a pastor I am often privileged to hear people's secret struggles with sin and their private prayers for cleansing. I have heard many broken people cry out to God in words that echo Psalm 51. For some, their tormenting sin has been pride. For others, it's a refusal to forgive others. Or it's drunkenness. Or adultery. Or greed. Or... If I haven't hit your particular sin, then you can fill in the details. As you think of the sins that devastate your soul, don't you yearn for a clean heart and a right spirit?

This is exactly what God gives us when we confess our sins to him. He will purify us from our sins and we will be clean; he will wash us and we will be whiter than snow.[3] Remember the promise of 1 John 1:9: "If we confess our sins, he who is faithful and just will forgive us our sins and *cleanse us from all unrighteousness*" (NRSV).

Benefit Three: Confession Enables Us to Experience the New Creation
Once we have put our faith in Jesus Christ, we begin to live in the new creation that will be complete only when God's kingdom fully comes. The Spirit of God dwells within us as a promise of the future. But in the present we are not completely free from sin even though its ultimate claim upon our lives has been annulled through the Cross. Thus we pray,

Create in me a clean heart, O God.
Renew a right spirit within me....
Restore to me again the joy of your salvation,
and make me willing to obey you. (Psalm 51:10,12)

The Hebrew verb that occurs in the phrase "*Create* in me a clean heart" is the same verb we find in Genesis 1:1, "In the beginning God *created* the heavens and the earth." When we ask the Lord to create in us a clean heart, we aren't looking for a temporary fix, something to tide us over for a while. We're seeking to be remade from the inside out. As this happens we delight in the joy of God's salvation and discover a renewed desire to obey him.

CONFESSION, FORGIVENESS, AND TRUTHFUL LIVING

As we have already seen, confessing our sins requires that we confront the hard truth that we'd rather avoid. When we confess, we speak the truth about our sin without trying to spin ourselves out of culpability. This does not tell the entire story of the relationship between confession and truthfulness, however. Confession not only requires truthfulness, but it also encourages our growth into greater truthfulness.

David recognized this in Psalm 51. After admitting his sin to God and asking for a clean heart, he continued, "Restore to me again the joy of your salvation, and make me willing to obey you. *Then I will teach your ways* to sinners, and they will return to you" (verses 12-13). As long as we are stuck in our sin and the denial that keeps us from confession, we will be a poor conduit of God's truth. But when, through confession, we have been renewed and restored, then we will be able to communicate divine truth effectively so that sinners will repent. Part of what makes our postconfession communication effective is our humility. When we have dealt with the truth of our sin and thrown ourselves upon God's mercy, we won't be likely to speak with arrogance.

Confession also prepares us for truthful living because it requires us to tackle some of the toughest truth of all, the truth of who we are as sinful people. Confession is like boot camp for truthfulness. If you can deal honestly with the truth about yourself that you'd rather avoid, then you're emotionally ready to engage still more truth.

Most important, confession removes the barrier that separates us from the God of truth. When we admit our sin to God, we experience forgiveness through Christ and are restored to intimate fellowship with God. Thus we are able to become more truthful not because of our own striving, but because God has drawn us near to himself.

TRUTHFULNESS IN THE CONFESSING COMMUNITY

Confession of sin augments our truthfulness not only as individuals but also as a community of faith. In a world filled with harsh accusations and devious excuses, the church stands apart as a place where people can tell the truth about their failures—or at least that's how it *should* be. I'll admit that churches can become pretentious parades where members flaunt their self-righteousness to impress their friends. How far this is from the biblical vision of the church as a community where we confess our sins to one another and pray for one another so that we may be healed (see James 5:16).

When we as Christians confess our sins corporately, we rejoice not only in our forgiveness but also in the freedom that comes from facing together the truth we'd rather avoid. I experienced this sort of freedom in my first year as pastor of Irvine Presbyterian Church. The church had a tradition of gathering annually for a special worship service that involved corporate confession. As pastor I was privileged to take part in this service.

Each person in the congregation received a piece of paper on which to write down his or her sins. Children who were too young to write drew pictures. Some people finished in a couple of minutes; others wrote for much longer, sometimes filling more than one piece of paper. When we finished, we folded our slips of paper, wrote our names on the outside, and came to the front of the sanctuary. There we faced a large wooden cross placed on the floor. In turn, we each nailed our "sins" to the cross.

As I participated in this service, I was flooded with many thoughts and feelings. I felt the power of nailing my sins to the cross and realized that, through this symbolic act, this is exactly what happened to Jesus for my sake. But I was also struck by the shared nature of our confession. Though I didn't know what others had written, I watched them confess by writing and pounding. Children so young that they needed their parents' help confessed, as did parents so old that they needed their children's help. With paper, hammer, and nail we agreed together that we "all have sinned and fall short of the glory of God" (Romans 3:23, NIV).

In this moment of shared confession, I was freed. I didn't have to be the perfect pastor. I didn't have to pretend as if my life were flawless. I could be honest about my struggle with sin, even as I could be open about the blessings of new life in Christ. Those who joined me in admitting their sins made it easier for me to do so, and I expect the reverse was also true.

But that wasn't the end of our journey into freedom. After we had all finished with the nailing, two worship leaders came to the front. Taking a slip of paper from the cross, they read the name on the outside and stated, "Mike, your sins are forgiven." "Lisa, your sins are forgiven." It took quite awhile for each person to receive the good news of forgiveness in Christ, but it was worth the wait. I'll never forget when my associate pastor Larry turned to me and said, "Mark, your sins are forgiven." No one had ever said that to me before in such a direct, personal way. I heard the truth of God's forgiveness and knew it was for me.

After the service, I sensed striking tenderness in the congregation. We had shared together the tragic truth of our sinfulness and the glorious truth of our forgiveness. How could our interactions be silly or superficial? In fact our conversations that evening were earnest and heartfelt. Choosing to face, rather than avoid, the hard truth about ourselves bound us together as a family of forgiven sinners, as people who didn't have to hide from God or from one another. Reconciled to God and to one another, we were empowered to live with greater truthfulness. The truth had set us free.

DIVINE TRAINING
IN TRUTHFULNESS

LEARNING FROM THE MASTER OF TRUTH

Willard Van Orman Quine. This name still sends a shiver down my spine.

I first heard of W. V. O. Quine at the beginning of my freshman year in college. He was famous—or, I should say, infamous—for having failed almost half of his students in a deductive logic class. One-third of the students washed out by the midterm, having done so poorly by that point that there was no reason for them to continue. When they complained to the college administration that Professor Quine was too tough, the educator insisted the fault was not his own, but was a result of lowered admissions standards. Take that, you whiners!

You may wonder if Professor Quine was reprimanded for failing half of his class. Was he threatened with losing his job for being an ineffective teacher? Hardly. You see, W. V. O. Quine was one of the most highly acclaimed philosophers of the last century. In his field of mathematical logic and the philosophy of logic, Quine was virtually peerless. Yet he seemed unable to pass along his expertise in logic to many of his students.

Because I planned to major in philosophy, I was required to take deductive logic from none other than Professor Quine. There was no way to avoid the Grim Reaper of the philosophy department. I hoped and prayed I wouldn't be consumed in the fiery furnace of Quine's logic class.

When I began deductive logic, I felt a combination of genuine fear, firm resolution, and respectful awe. From the start of the first class, I began to figure out why so many of my predecessors had failed. Professor Quine, a master of logic, was not a master of teaching. He read his lectures from yellowed, dog-eared three-by-five-inch cards that suggested his presentations had been written decades earlier. Moreover, he would not answer questions from the floor. If we had questions, we had to write them down and turn them in. At the next class Professor Quine would give an answer, reading it from—you guessed it—a three-by-five card.

As you might imagine, the required textbooks for this class were written by none other than W. V. O. Quine. His books were by far the most helpful aspect of the course, though certain passages were difficult to interpret. For example, consider this morsel of wisdom from his *Philosophy of Logic:*

> What are best regarded as true and false are not propositions but sentence tokens, or sentences if they are eternal. The desire for a non-linguistic truth vehicle comes of not appreciating that the truth predicate has precisely the purpose of reconciling the mention of linguistic forms with an interest in the objective world.[1]

If we couldn't understand what this meant, we wouldn't get much help from Professor Quine.

What a sadly ironic scenario! The brilliant logician struggled to teach beginning logic. The esteemed commentator on logical truth couldn't train his students to become truthful. With plenty of hard work during one semester, I was able to become proficient enough in deductive logic to pass the course. I learned to manipulate logical symbols so that I could determine whether certain statements were true or not according to the strict standards of mathematical logic.

WHO WILL TRAIN US IN TRUTH?

Deductive logic was the toughest class of my academic career. But the challenge of learning how to evaluate symbolic truth in one semester does not compare in difficulty with the challenge of learning how to live as people of truth in the real world. After forty-five years I'm still trying to become a truthful person. I don't think I've flunked Truthful Living 101 yet, but I can't claim to have mastered the course material either. In a sinful, spinful world, learning to live in complete honesty is a lifelong challenge.

This raises obvious questions. Can anyone teach us this subject? Or is life like my deductive logic class, where you must teach yourself if you're going to learn anything?

When it comes to the truth, there is an obvious potential teacher—God, the One who is revealed to us as the Truthful Trinity. Wouldn't it be wonderful if God would design a course syllabus to train us in truthfulness? That's what David sought in Psalm 86: "Teach me your ways, O LORD, that I may live according to your truth!" (verse 11). Similarly, in Psalm 25 David prayed, "Show me the path where I should walk, O LORD; point out the right road for me to follow. Lead me by your truth and teach me" (verses 4-5).

These are sensible, heartfelt requests. But will God really help fallible, deceitful people like us learn to live truthfully? Or is he more like Professor Quine, a master of truth who is so far ahead of the rest of us that he can't pass on his mastery?

I have good news for you. Scripture makes it clear that God won't flunk you at the midterm, even if you deserve it. In multiple ways the Lord answers the prayers of our hearts—as he answered David's prayer—by leading us in his truth and helping us walk in it. Scripture reveals at least four ways God trains us.

The Training of Negative Consequences

First, God trains us through the negative consequences of our behavior. In God's providence, our choice of a lie over the truth often leads directly to negative results, and these results teach us to be truthful. Paul's letter to the Romans reveals that humans "deliberately chose to believe lies," rejecting "what they knew was the truth about God" (1:25). What was the result of choosing falsehood? People "suffered within themselves the penalty they so richly deserved" (1:27). In other words, sinful choices led naturally to negative consequences.

A popular story illustrates the negative consequences that can follow from lying. Two students at Duke University were taking introductory chemistry from Professor Bonk, renowned for having taught this course for decades. They excelled in the course, so much so that on the weekend before the final they dedicated themselves to partying rather than studying. But dissipation caught up with them, and they slept through their chemistry exam.

Approaching Professor Bonk, the students pleaded for mercy. They claimed they had been out of town during the weekend and had had a flat tire on the return trip. The flat prevented them from returning in time for the test. The professor graciously allowed the two students another chance to take the exam.

When they showed up the next day for the final, the prof put them in two separate rooms and gave them each a test booklet. The first problem on the first page was easy enough and worth five points—5 percent of the exam grade. Each student quickly aced that problem and moved on to the next page. There they read, "95 points: Which tire?"[2]

Though negative consequences often follow lying, God did not create the world so that painful results ensue immediately. Sometimes liars appear to beat the rap, at least for a while. Even Professor Bonk's students had an outside chance of guessing correctly, or at least guessing identically, and passing chemistry in spite of their deception. Sometimes liars make a fortune in business or get elected to high office. The negative consequences of lying can take years to appear. Thus, we aren't going to become truthful people without additional help. Moreover, we'd hope these consequences might be a last resort, not the first step in our training. Does God help us live truthfully before we experience the negative consequences that ultimately result from lying?

The Training of Scripture

Even as Professor Quine wrote a textbook to teach logic, so God has inspired a Book to teach living. As we read through the Bible, God's textbook, we learn how to tell and how to live the truth.

In many passages Scripture regularly commends truthfulness and condemns falsehood. Even though some exceptional stories show how people lied to accomplish some worthy goal—such as the lies Rahab told to protect the spies in Joshua 2—scriptural teaching repeatedly affirms the superiority of truthfulness. The Ten Commandments instruct us not to "testify falsely against [our] neighbor" (Exodus 20:16), a directive that applies literally to a legal context but, by implication, underlines the value of truthful speech in general.

According to the Psalms, the people who may approach God's holy presence are those who "do what is right, speaking the truth from sincere hearts" (15:2). Liars, on the contrary, are those whom "the LORD detests" (5:6). The book of Proverbs warns, "A false witness will not go unpunished, and a liar will be destroyed" (19:9). Ephesians calls us to "put away all falsehood" and "tell your neighbor the truth" (4:25). Included among a New Testament list of "godless and sinful" people are "murderers, fornicators, sodomites, slave traders, liars, [and] perjurers" (1 Timothy 1:9-10, NRSV). Next time you're tempted to lie, think about whether you want to be included in that list!

In addition to clear commands and prohibitions, the Scriptures provide a much more compelling commendation of truthfulness: the revelation of God's own nature. When we realize that God is full of truth, then our desire to be truthful increases dramatically because we yearn to be like the One in whose image we were created. The Bible reveals a vision of the truthful God that moves those who love God to imitate divine truthfulness. As we seek to become more like God, we will necessarily live truthfully and avoid deception.

To help us keep away from the negative consequences of lying, God's Word leads us into truthfulness both through instruction and example and, ultimately, through the revelation of God's truthful nature. Yet God provides still more help in our growth toward truthful living.

The Training of God's Spirit of Truth

In the gospel of John, Jesus explains that the Holy Spirit helps us to be truthful. The Spirit "will guide [us] into all truth" (16:13), by teaching us "everything" and reminding us of what Jesus taught (14:26). Thus, the same Spirit who filled Jesus with divine power dwells within us to train us in truthfulness.

How does this spiritual training happen? First and most important, the

Spirit helps us understand and embrace biblical teaching, including instruction on truthfulness. The same Spirit who once inspired the writers of the Bible, leading them to write the truth and nothing but the truth, inspires our understanding of God's divine truth. Thus, unlike Professor Quine who wrote impressive books but couldn't explain their meaning to ordinary people, the Holy Spirit helps ordinary believers grasp the truth of Spirit-inspired Scripture.

Second, the Spirit works in concert with our consciences, saying an inner "Amen" when we are truthful and whispering "uh-oh" when we are not. In writing to the Romans, Paul stated, "In the presence of Christ, I speak with utter truthfulness—I do not lie—and my conscience and the Holy Spirit confirm that what I am saying is true" (9:1). In an ideal world our consciences would be enough to keep us on the path of truth. But neither the world nor our consciences are ideal. Both have been corrupted by sin. Yet God does not leave us in our sin-induced ignorance. He speaks within our hearts, trumping the often confused voice of our consciences with the clarion call of his Spirit.

One day when I was working at Hollywood Presbyterian Church, a man I'll call Tom arrived at the church campus completely out of breath and insisting that he see a pastor right away. Tom was completely disheveled, sweaty, and panting, his shirttail hanging loose. I wondered if he had been mugged. Once we found a quiet place to talk, Tom poured out his story.

"Pastor," he said, "I'm an elder in my church, a husband to a wonderful wife, and a father of three children. But I almost threw it all away. You see, I fell in love with a woman at work. At first we just flirted and it seemed harmless, but soon our feelings for each other grew. We began sneaking out for lunch together. Of course, we covered our tracks well, lying to our coworkers and our spouses. We had never become sexually involved, but we decided that today would be the day to start. So we got a hotel room nearby. When we began to get undressed, I looked over on the nightstand and saw one of those Gideon Bibles. At that moment it was as if God talked to me. I realized that I was going to ruin my life and hurt all the people I love the most. So I grabbed my clothes and ran away. As I was running down the street, I saw your church steeple, so

I ran over here. I need your help. I don't want to be unfaithful to my wife. I don't want to sneak around anymore and lie to everybody."

As Tom and I talked further, I asked if he had shared any of this with people from his own church. "No," he explained, "I was too afraid of what people might think of me."

He continued to unburden his heart, repeatedly going back to that moment in the hotel room. "I can't believe what God did for me. It's like I heard his voice. He saved me from ruining my life."

Though our stories may not be quite as dramatic as Tom's, we, too, have heard the inner voice of the Spirit cheering us on when we're choosing to live rightly, and reproving us when we're sinning. For weeks Tom had chosen to ignore the Spirit's conviction as he continued to weave his web of deceit. But the Spirit didn't quit. Finally, with Tom at the brink of disaster, God almost shouted at him, and by grace Tom was able to hear.

When we live deceptively, we choose to ignore the Spirit's pleading, the testimony of Scripture, and even the likelihood that our lies will lead to negative consequences. When we try to go it alone, as Tom did for far too long, we frequently can't muster the strength to avoid sinning. But God has not left us alone. He has given us Christian community so that we might be strengthened for righteous and truthful living.

The Training of a Truthful Community

When we put our faith in Jesus, the Holy Spirit joins us to the body of Christ so that we might strengthen and encourage one another. As we saw earlier, the church is "the pillar and support of the truth," a community where we " 'tell [our] neighbor the truth' because we belong to each other" (1 Timothy 3:15; Ephesians 4:25). Thus, we are to be a countercultural community in a world filled with deception, a spiritual family in which we urge one another to grow in the truth. No matter how difficult this kind of growth may be in a hostile world, we will find the strength to live in complete honesty when we don't try to do it alone.

In 1984 a dear family friend decided she wanted to run a marathon. Even though Nancy had been a faithful jogger for many years, she had never tackled a full marathon. Someone suggested she join a track club, where focused training and regular encouragement would help her fulfill her dream.

Nancy joined a club near where she worked, and when she returned from her first workout, I asked her how it went. "Awful" was her immediate response. "Terrible. I think I'm the worst runner in the world. The other people in the club run three times faster than I do. They run; I just waddle. Maybe I should quit the club."

"It can't be that bad," I said, trying to be reassuring. "Give it another try. I'm sure it will be better."

So Nancy went back, but she returned just as discouraged as before. Still trying to be positive, I told Nancy I'd go with her the next time to see what was wrong.

When we arrived at the college where the club trained, I had a hunch why Nancy felt so out of place. As an avid track fan, I associated Santa Monica City College with one particular club. Sure enough, Nancy had joined the Santa Monica Track Club. She was working out with the best runners in the world— literally. Members of the club included Carl Lewis and Evelyn Ashford, both of whom won Olympic gold medals in 1984. As I watched Nancy run around the track at a respectable pace, the others were indeed going three times faster than she was. No wonder she was feeling a bit outclassed! I waved Nancy over to the side of the track and explained: "They do run a lot faster than you do, Nancy, because *they're the fastest runners in the world!* Next to them, we'd all look pretty pathetic. So don't compare yourself to them. Just keep on going and you'll be fine."

Feeling relieved, Nancy kept training. The coach and other members welcomed and encouraged her. Being part of the club helped. Though Nancy never won a gold medal in the Olympics, she did complete her first marathon in an impressive time.

The church of Jesus Christ should be like that track club when it comes to training in truthfulness. Within the church are some who have walked with the

Lord for decades, saints whose souls have been shaped through years of faithful discipleship. They are gold medalists in truthful living. Their expertise is not meant to discourage others, but to inspire and teach them. Some of us will run around the track of truth more slowly than others, but in the community of Christ, we will find help to keep going and to grow in our ability.

I've seen this dimension of Christian fellowship countless times. For instance, a high-school girl in my church shared with her small group that she had been smoking marijuana. Within this circle of trusted sisters in Christ, she felt the freedom to be honest about her struggle. The group helped her realize that she needed to tell her parents what was going on, but she was understandably afraid of how they might react. So the group prayed for her faithfully and encouraged her to come clean with her folks. When it was time for the dreaded conversation, her small group leader joined her. The tangible support of her leader gave this girl the confidence to be honest with her parents, who were finally empowered to help her overcome her dependence on drugs.

When I think of how we can help one another grow in truthfulness, I remember a retreat with the men from my church. It began on Friday evening with lots of hilarity, worship, and solid Bible teaching—all of it quite delightful. Each man was assigned to a small group, a place to share our lives and pray for one another. The small groups were friendly but superficial. Most men don't readily share what's really going on in their lives even with close friends, not to mention with casual acquaintances.

The next morning after the Bible study, one of the leaders in the church shared openly how he had been struggling in his Christian walk. He risked moving beyond generalities and divulged in some detail where he found it most difficult to honor the Lord. In particular, work-related situations had sparked the fire of lust within him. Although he sought to be faithful to his wife, he was really struggling, and he asked for our prayers. He demonstrated gutsy honesty, trusting that we would hold what he shared in confidence.

In the small-group discussion that followed, I was astounded at the transformation of our conversation. Men ventured to open their hearts. One man divulged his shame over his lack of professional accomplishments. Another man whom we had always assumed was a Christian admitted that he never really had trusted Christ for his salvation. What had transformed the quality of sharing in our group? Obviously, it was the example of the church leader who told the truth about his own weakness. His courage *encouraged* others, literally. It gave them *courage*.

The greater openness in our group led to deeper prayer and mutual love. We poured out our hearts to God for help with the struggles in our lives. We pleaded with God to set the one man free from his shame and to help the other come to faith. The next day, as the retreat was drawing to a close, the man who was not a Christian stood up to share. With tears in his eyes, he explained that for the first time in his life he truly understood the gospel and put his faith in Jesus Christ. What began that weekend continues, as this man walks faithfully with Christ today. How grateful I am for the brave honesty of the man whose openness helped the rest of us share our lives with one another. (The impact of Christian community upon our truthfulness will be the focus of the next chapter.)

SITTING AT THE FEET OF THE MASTER

God seeks to train us in truthfulness. Unlike my former logic professor, God is a Master Teacher who excels at passing along his expertise. Through negative consequences, Scripture, the Holy Spirit, and Christian community, God instructs and shapes us to be truthful people.

Yet God does not impose his mastery upon us. He wants willing students; indeed, he seeks loving children. But many of us resist embracing the humility required to learn from God. We want to be masters, not disciples; experts, not beginners. This is especially true for those of us who usually find ourselves in the position of the teacher, the one with all the answers.

When I was beginning my ministry at Hollywood Presbyterian Church, a man named John Holland offered to train me in public speaking. John was an accomplished actor and an instructor in speech at Fuller Seminary. He had a few private students whom he charged a princely fee. But, as a member of the

Hollywood church, John was willing to work with me free of charge. Recognizing John's mastery, I gladly accepted his offer.

Learning from John was not easy on my ego, however. He didn't waste time smoothing his criticisms. As I'd be reading some portion of Scripture, John would often interrupt me with such cheery comments as "Stop! That's awful! Read it again, and get the meaning this time!" When I finally succeeded, John would praise me. Knowing his no-nonsense approach to teaching, I greatly valued his praise.

As I think back on those sessions, I feel abundantly grateful. John helped me in many ways. I continue to be influenced by his teaching even though he has long since gone to be with the Lord. But, as I remember my hours at John's feet, I feel more than gratitude. I also cringe because I can still feel the discomfort of my humility before him. Yet, if I had it to do all over again, I'd be right back there under John's authority.

The God of the universe, the Truthful Trinity, wants to tutor you in the truth. He offers a combination of private lessons and group classes. Though his instruction is invaluable, he will teach you free of charge. The benefits will be priceless. So what will be your answer to God's invitation? Will you sit at the feet of the Master of truth?

TRUTHFUL COMMUNITY

Don't Even Try to Go It Alone

L ying isn't the exclusive domain of adults. It begins early in life when our mothers ask us if we took an extra cookie, hit our little brother, or broke the lamp. And the temptation to evade the full truth doesn't let up as we grow older. Just ask a teenager.

All teenagers face the challenge of whether to lie to their parents. The situations vary, of course, but the opportunities are endless. There's homework, friends, dating, drugs, drinking, sex, money, and jobs. You can probably add a few more items to the list. No matter how the details may vary, the challenge ends up more or less the same: Should I lie to my parents?

Once, when I was a high-school senior, I arrived home two hours after my parents were expecting me. To my relief, they were asleep. Somehow I managed to sneak into my room without waking them. Safe!—or so I thought. But the next morning my dad asked me, "Mark, when did you get home last night?" In a flash I calculated my options. I could tell the truth and risk receiving some sort of discipline. I could lie and claim to have come in earlier, thus avoiding the negative consequences of telling the truth, unless my parents had been awake at the hour I claimed to have arrived home, in which case the consequences would be far worse. I could try to fudge things altogether and simply say, "I don't know," but this was really a more devious lie because I knew exactly when I got home, and it was way beyond my curfew.

Standing face to face with my dad, I wasn't able to lie. I told the truth and accepted the outcome. But I might have been less honest if I had been able to talk it over with my friends. I'm sure some of them would have urged me to finagle: "Just tell your dad that you didn't look at the clock. That way he can't nail you. Everybody does things like this." Indeed, just about everybody *does* twist the truth at times, and that makes it doubly hard to tell the complete truth when it might be costly to do so.

We live in a world that provides little support for truthfulness. To be sure, as we grow up our parents and teachers tell us we shouldn't lie. But they sometimes send contradictory messages. Professor Robert Feldman, whose study of lying I mentioned in previous chapters, explains:

> We teach our children that honesty is the best policy, but we also tell them it's polite to pretend they like a birthday gift they've been given. Kids get a very mixed message regarding the practical aspects of lying, and it has an impact on how they behave as adults.[1]

In countless ways our world commends deception. A man says to his colleague, "Just slip in that extra receipt with your expense report. Your boss will never know." Or a woman coaches her friend, "Don't tell your husband what you spent on that dress. He'll never find out." Of course, the news media are filled with stories of liars who get away with it and spinners who make millions of dollars because they're so adept at shading the truth. Moreover, we are bombarded with differing opinions—often outright contradictions—on the issues of the day. One pundit claims to know the real truth. Another argues that the opposing view is, in fact, true. For instance, do you feel confident that you grasp the real truth of what's going on in the Middle East? Complexity and contradiction abound when it comes to this confusing region of the world and its endless problems. With experts countering one another's views on virtually every point, it's easy to become perplexed, or even to doubt that truth can be found at all.

According to Walter Truett Anderson in his book *The Truth About the Truth*, the plethora of ideas, perspectives, and worldviews in our multicultural world leads us to question the very nature of truth. "Surrounded by so many truths,"

Anderson writes, "we can't help but revise our concept of truth itself: our beliefs about belief. More and more people become acquainted with the idea that, as philosopher Richard Rorty puts it, truth is made rather than found."[2]

Of course, most people don't read the technical treatises of Richard Rorty, but his views and those of other postmodern thinkers trickle down to ordinary folk through college lectures and newspaper opinion columns, through hit movies and talk radio. In the process, the idea that "truth is made rather than found" becomes a rationale for making up the truth as we go along. And, typically, it's a form of "truth" that suits our own interests perfectly.

If we find ourselves getting dizzy in a world of spin, how can we ever hope to become adept at speaking the truth, not to mention living it? How can we live in complete honesty when all around us the prevailing message hammers us with "Don't worry about lying. Nobody will ever find out. What is truth anyway?"

There isn't a simple answer to these questions. But one thing I know for sure, if you seek to be a person of truth in today's world, you can't do it alone. That's what Jesus affirmed in the gospel of John.

Truthful Community in the Prayer of Jesus

Jesus' prayer in John 17 offers an incisive diagnosis of our predicament. We who believe in Jesus have been set apart from the world by the truth of God. We have become strangers in a strange land, a land that once felt like home. Notice that God's truth—encapsulated in the gospel of Jesus Christ—is what makes us different from the world.

The world doesn't take kindly to the impact of truth. We no longer belong to the world because Jesus has given us God's sanctifying Word, so *the world hates us* (see John 17:14). Given the world's hatred, we might be tempted to withdraw to some isolated stronghold, far removed from the world and its deceit. But Jesus prayed specifically that his disciples will not be taken "out of the world" (17:15). In fact, even as the Father sent Jesus into the world, so Jesus has sent us. We have been sent as Jesus' representatives right into the midst of a world that despises us because we don't share its values.

What will help us withstand the pressure to conform to the ways of the world? Christian community is the answer. Throughout his prayer Jesus is not praying for Christians as separate individuals, but as a community of disciples. He has not sent you into the world as a Lone Ranger, but as part of a purposeful posse. Our togetherness as Christians is essential to our truthfulness. It's no coincidence that Jesus moves from praying about our separateness from the world to asking for our unity with one another:

> I am praying not only for these disciples but also for all who will ever
> believe in me because of their testimony. My prayer for all of them is
> that they will be one, just as you and I are one, Father. (John 17:20-21)

Jesus is not envisioning some fleeting esprit de corps, like school spirit that gets whipped up at homecoming. Indeed, he prays that we may be "completely one" even as Jesus is one with the Father (verses 22-23, NRSV). Now that's serious unity!

Jesus recognizes that, as people of truth, we have been set apart from the world that resents our differentness. We must not withdraw from this world, however, because Jesus has sent us into it as bearers of the truth. We have been set apart and sent, not as individuals, but as a community. Our unity in Christ will support, defend, and extend our truthfulness in a hostile world.

THE DIMENSIONS OF TRUTHFUL COMMUNITY

In Paul's letter to the Ephesians, we see a similar connection between Christian community and truthful living. The apostle urges us to "maintain the unity of the Spirit in the bond of peace" (4:3, NRSV), and he anchors this unity in the very oneness of God. As a unified people, we are to reject the trickery and deceit of our world in favor of "speaking the truth in love," so that we may "grow up in every way" into Christ (4:15, NRSV). Our countercultural truthfulness is both a feature of our life together and that which helps us grow into even greater unity as God's people.

Ephesians 4, like John 17, emphasizes our distinctness from the world. We must "throw off" the life of the world and "display a new nature...created in God's likeness" (verses 22,24). In light of this, Paul exclaimed, "So put away all falsehood and 'tell your neighbor the truth' because we belong to each other" (verse 25). Notice the rationale for our truthfulness: *because we belong to each other.* Since we have been joined together by God, we reject the lie and speak the truth. Truthfulness is a function of our life in community, even as it enhances that community. By standing together we will be empowered to *stand against* the falsehood of our world and to *stand for* the truthfulness of God. Like Jesus in John 17, Paul demonstrated the necessary connection between truthful living and Christian fellowship. If we seek to be people of truth, we must live out the truth as members of the body of Christ, as people set apart by God's truth and bound together in Christian unity.

In theory, the unifying power of truthful living has great appeal. The challenge comes when we try to put it into practice. If we are going to form churches that promote truthfulness in a deceitful world, what will be required of us? Following are five practical dimensions of truthful community, each of them necessary for living in complete honesty as the people of God.

1. The Community Must Promote Truthfulness

To encourage truth in the world around us, we must first be a community that promotes truthfulness in all aspects of life *within* the community. We should affirm one another when we tell the truth, especially when truth is told in a difficult circumstance. Likewise, if we recognize that a sister or brother is not being truthful, we ought to confront that person in private and in love (see Matthew 18:15). When a friend struggles with whether to tell the truth, we must encourage and pray for that person, even holding him or her accountable to do the right thing.

I'm in a small group with several pastors in my area. We regularly help one another to live truthfully in our ministries, our marriages, and our relationships with the Lord. Recently one member of the group was struggling with a leader in his congregation who was maligning him behind his back as well as criticizing him to his face. As this pastor wrestled with how to respond, we encouraged him to speak the truth in love, both with the critical individual and with the elders of his church, although we knew these would be difficult discussions. When we gathered for our next meeting, we checked in to see if our brother had acted as he had promised, and we were glad to hear that he had. Our fellowship together encouraged his truthfulness in a tough situation.

2. The Community Must Model Truthfulness

It won't do much good to urge one another to tell the truth if we're not doing it in our own lives. We need to model what we're encouraging others to do. If the fellow pastor in my accountability group, whom we encouraged to speak the truth, knew that the rest of us didn't do the same thing in our own ministries, I doubt he would have been persuaded to follow our counsel.

This commitment to model the life of truth to one another can be costly—literally. Several years ago my wife and I took my daughter to an expensive amusement park on her birthday. As it turned out, she had just passed an age marker that greatly increased the cost of her admission ticket. If Linda and I told a "little white lie," understating Kara's age by just one day, we'd save a bundle. But Kara, standing there bursting with pride that she was now a year older, would have heard us tell the lie. Not only would she have been angry that we denied her great chronological achievement, but she would have received a powerful message about the financial rewards of deception.

I know of parents who, when their children were young, repeatedly lied in situations like this just to save a few bucks. When checking into a hotel, they'd "forget" to mention they had their kids with them. Or they misrepresented their children's ages to get a discount. Kids aren't dimwits. They quickly pick up what parents really believe about truth, and this influences children's behavior much more than what their parents tell them about not lying.

I was blessed with truthful parents. I never remember my parents telling a lie either to me or to anyone else. Though they encouraged me to speak the truth, their example spoke more powerfully to me than their wise words.

Truthful living is important for our children, but it's equally important to other adults who observe our lives. When I was a young associate pastor at

Hollywood Presbyterian Church, I carefully scrutinized the example of my boss and mentor Lloyd Ogilvie. I saw Lloyd on good days and bad days, in times of joy and times of sorrow. He always spoke carefully, aware of the power of words either to build up or to tear down. But he never compromised the truth. He had the courage to say what needed to be said even when it was tough to say—and tough for the other person to hear.

I'll never forget the conversation we had when I first told him about my interest in being called to pastor Irvine Presbyterian Church. Lloyd could have pumped me up with falsehoods to encourage me, or he could have twisted the truth to try to keep me from leaving Hollywood Presbyterian. Instead, he opened his heart to me, sharing how much he wished I would stay on his staff but affirming that the Lord's will was what mattered most. He told me that I'd be a great senior pastor, even though a part of him hoped I'd remain as an associate for a few more years. I know this was a hard conversation for Lloyd, as it was for me. But his honesty made all the difference. I still consider that conversation to be one of the watershed moments of my life.

When I began my ministry as a senior pastor, I found myself imitating Lloyd's honesty both consciously and unconsciously. When I struggled to say hard things to a staff person, I'd think about what Lloyd would have done. His example gave me a pattern to follow and the courage to speak the truth even when I felt afraid.

Do the people who consider you to be a role model learn truthfulness from you? If you're a parent, does your example consistently guide your children into truthful living? What about your employees, your classmates, or the kids you coach on the soccer field? Do you model complete honesty in your words and your deeds?

3. The Community Must Discern the Truth in Difficult Situations

In addition to encouraging and modeling truthfulness, we must be a community of discernment, a place where we help one another clarify what it means to speak the truth in love when the truth of the situation isn't obvious. Sometimes we honestly don't know what we ought to say. For example, if a parent of young children has a life-threatening disease, what ought to be said to the children and when? Or when a relative commits suicide, how should family members explain the tragic death to outsiders? Or what should members of a small group say to the wounded group member who dominates every discussion with her pain? When we face tough questions like these, it helps to have wise brothers and sisters in Christ with whom to discern not just what is true, but how the truth should be communicated.

Sometimes we are reticent to speak the truth because of the complexity of a situation or because of our own limited perspective. People often come to me as a pastor for help in discerning the truth that needs to be spoken. For instance, several members of my congregation have served in political office. Often they have to speak definitively with respect to complicated issues. At times they have asked me to be a sounding board for them as they try to determine what they ought to say about a given issue. They're committed to speaking the truth once they figure out what it is. I try to help them discern the truth.

Many times I have found similar support in my effort to be a pastoral leader in my church. For instance, there have been times when a staff person is not meeting my expectations. I know I need to communicate with that person, but I'm not exactly sure what to say. Is there really a performance problem, or are my expectations unrealistic? In these situations I'm grateful to share the leadership of my church with a board of elders. When I bring my confusion to them, they help me see clearly so that I might speak truthfully. The discernment that comes from the body of Christ is a precious gift of God.

Of course, you probably don't have a board of elders at your disposal, but if you are living as an active member of the body of Christ, you will have trusted brothers or sisters to whom you can turn for advice. If your spouse is a Christian, he or she is another ready source of insight. I'd strongly recommend that you rely on the wisdom of a small group of believers who know you well. My wife, for example, meets each Friday with a couple of Christian women. They share life's challenges together, offering lots of empathy and, when needed, wise counsel. If you are not part of such a group, now is the time to join one, or even to form one.[3]

4. Community Members Must Share the Truth About Themselves

If we are going to be a truthful community, then the church must be a place where we can share the truth about ourselves, even the secrets that bring us shame. This includes the personal failures that steal our peace and the hidden sins that enslave us. These things, if left unspoken, have the power to discourage, depress, and defeat us. By keeping them locked inside, we cut ourselves off from the healing, forgiveness, and peace God offers. Yet the thought of sharing these secrets with others can be scary. We'll never do it unless we feel confident that our secrets will be treated with respect and that we will be treated with love after admitting our flaws and weaknesses.

Several years ago a member of my church made an appointment with me. Bill began by saying that he wanted to share something he had never told anyone in the church. It took a long time before he was able to divulge his secret: He had struggled for years with depression and had finally found help through medication. Yet he felt ashamed, both because he had been depressed and because he was taking Prozac. He believed that he was the only person in the church who struggled with such things. I tried to listen sensitively, to reassure him both of God's love and of the fact that he wasn't alone in his battle with depression. Because I needed to keep confidences, I couldn't tell him the names of others like him, but I mentioned that there were many.

A couple of days later another man came to see me for exactly the same reason. Jeff also felt ashamed and alone in his battle with depression. I had a strange sense of déjà vu as I attempted to reassure him of God's love and the fact that he was not alone. I couldn't help but wish that somehow I could get Jeff and Bill to form a prayer partnership.

The next Sunday morning as I gazed out into the congregation I saw Bill and Jeff sitting right next to each other. How I wished I could stop my sermon and say to them, "Look, this brother right here is just like you. Why don't you become prayer partners? You need each other!" But I didn't do that for obvious reasons. I fear both men probably thought the other looked so good on the outside that he must have had everything together in his life.

A year ago I shared the story of Bill and Jeff in a sermon. (The story is true, by the way, but the names are fictitious.) Right after the sermon one of my elders told me, "I've had the same problem as Bill and Jeff. For years I suffered with depression, but I finally found relief by taking Prozac, and I'm feeling much better now. I'm not afraid for others to know. You can always use my name if you wish. You can tell people to call me, or I'll gladly call them." Courage like this will help our church become a place where we can tell even the embarrassing truths about ourselves so that we might experience more of God's healing.

Of course, there's a risk in this kind of openness, and that's what keeps many of us silent. We're afraid that if we share who we really are, people will judge us or reject us. But we won't become a community where we can share ourselves unless we have created a place of safety, a place where we trust one another because we have been faithful (troth-full) to others when they have been truthful about themselves. Furthermore, until we individually confront the truth of our own sinfulness, we won't be able to respond to the sins of others with grace, wisdom, and humility. We'll either be judgmental, as if we are better than others, or too permissive, failing to hold up God's standards for righteousness. But once we recognize our own failures and brokenness, and once we have been forgiven and mended through God's grace, then we'll be able to receive one another gracefully.

Do you struggle with judgmentalism? Do you readily condemn the failures of others while all too easily rationalizing your own? If so, you need the freedom that comes from admitting this tendency to the Lord and asking for both his forgiveness and his help in being more gracious to others. Don't be one of those people who is so eager to point out the speck of sawdust in the eye of another while neglecting the lumberyard in his or her own eyes (see Matthew 7:3-5)! There is great joy in being able to offer freely to others the same grace God has freely given you.

All of us struggle with hard things, and, tragically, we struggle even more with sharing them so that we might receive prayer, encouragement, and support. As a pastor I hear the secrets that people are afraid to share with others. These commonly include spiritual doubt, prayerlessness, loneliness, substance abuse, depression, sexual temptation or sin, marital unhappiness, worry about finances, and feeling like a failure at work, in the family, or in school. Each one of us needs to be in a Christian community where we are free to share these struggles so that we might share in God's power over them. If we have the guts to be open with others, we'll help one another discover freedom and healing. And we ourselves will enjoy the blessings of freedom and healing in our own lives.

5. The Community Must Tell Us the Truth About Ourselves

If we are to be a fully truthful community, then we will be open to hearing the truth about ourselves, even when it's difficult. We will be willing to be confronted when we are wrong so that we might change and grow. Of course this assumes that we have significant relationships with brothers and sisters in Christ who will risk telling us this truth. Truth telling of this sort takes courage on both sides of the dialogue. And, needless to say, it is a time when the truth must be spoken in love.

I was in college when I first found myself on the receiving end of one such confrontation. In my young-adult years, I was habitually late getting to appointments, often up to twenty or thirty minutes. I felt rather embarrassed about my lateness, but my embarrassment didn't translate into changed behavior.

One day a Christian friend named John said he had something important to share with me. He began by telling me several things he appreciated about me and reassuring me that he cared deeply for me as a brother in Christ. I know he meant well with this introduction, but it really made me nervous. Finally, John got to the punch line. He told me that my habitual lateness to our Bible study group was really a problem. He said that it was unkind and disrespectful to others in the group and that it was time for a change. John and the other members of the group were committed to helping me be on time. They would pray for me and hold me accountable. I didn't especially like hearing those things, but I knew he was right. Once I got over my defensiveness, I was grateful for John's gutsy honesty.

A COMMUNITY CENTERED IN THE MOST IMPORTANT
TRUTH OF ALL

There is one other crucial aspect of being a truthful community, perhaps the most essential and wonderful aspect of all, but one we might easily overlook. *As disciples of Jesus Christ, we have the privilege of continually reminding one another of the truth of the gospel.* We hold up the truth that we are saved not by our good deeds or good intentions, but by God's grace. In the community of Christ, we hear that our sins are forgiven because Christ bore them for us on the cross. We celebrate the astounding truth of Romans 8 that

> nothing can ever separate us from [Christ's] love. Death can't, and life can't. The angels can't, and the demons can't. Our fears for today, our worries about tomorrow, and even the powers of hell can't keep God's love away. Whether we are high above the sky or in the deepest ocean, nothing in all creation will ever be able to separate us from the love of God that is revealed in Christ Jesus our Lord. (verses 38-39)

Did you catch this? Once you have put your trust in Jesus as your Savior, *nothing* will be able to separate you from God's love. Not your spiritual doubt or prayerlessness. Not your loneliness, substance abuse, or depression. Not sexual sin or your unhappiness in your marriage or your worry about finances. Not your feelings of failure. None of these will separate you from God's love in Christ.

This is good news. Indeed, it's God's good news for you. But it's not for you alone. God wants you to share it with others. You have the privilege of telling others the truth about God's love in Christ, and what a privilege this is. As a pastor I regularly get to do this in preaching and in counseling, in praying for people and in offering the sacraments. It's one of the aspects of pastoring I love the most. But it's your calling as well as mine. And it's your blessing as well as mine.

As you seek to contribute to the truthfulness of your Christian community, let the good news of the gospel flow from your lips like cool, refreshing water from an artesian spring. Remind your brothers and sisters of the most important truth of all: that "nothing in all creation will ever be able to separate us from the love of God that is revealed in Christ Jesus our Lord" (Romans 8:39).

SPEAK GENTLY AND BURY
YOUR BIG STICK

Don't Be an Obnoxious Christian

Most of the time I'm proud to be a member of the church of Jesus Christ. But every now and then I cringe at being associated with Christians who are, frankly, obnoxious.

Sometimes this happens when I'm listening to talk radio. Some secular, in-your-face shock jock is saying outlandish things, trying to get a rise out of people, especially those who hold "outdated puritanical values." The ploy works like a charm. A caller comes on the air and announces in a strident voice, "I'm a Christian, and…." I wince in anticipation of what's coming next. The combination of the person's angry tone with the assertion "I'm a Christian" rarely turns out well. Inevitably, the caller, hooked by the harsh tone of the talk-show host, blasts away with white-hot fury. Though I often agree with the caller's position on the issues, I'm nevertheless embarrassed by the tone of the presentation. Good intentions and godly truth are lost in a torrent of angry arrogance.

Sometimes prideful communication flows from the *other* side of the microphone as well. Recently I was listening to a couple of Christian talk-show hosts. They sounded so cocky and self-assured, as if they had cornered the market on truth. And, even though I agreed with their ideas, I found myself embarrassed by their tone. Listening to their program, you could easily conclude that God had pulled them aside and entrusted them with special insider information that they were now generous enough to share with the rest of us.

It's often said that we react most negatively to things in others that we dislike about ourselves. I must confess that this helps explain my revulsion to arrogance in Christians. I, too, find it natural to ride in on my theological white horse, thinking that I'm saving spiritual peons from their ignorance. Sadly, I can sound just as obnoxious as any radio show host.

I first realized this discomforting truth when I was in graduate school. As part of my work in a seminar, I was assigned to respond to a paper presented by another student. The topic had to do with the interpretation of a tiny passage in *The Temple Scroll,* one of the Dead Sea Scrolls. After the other student read his paper, I presented my response. Meticulously, I showed the flaws in his argument. After I finished, I silently applauded myself for my brilliance.

For some reason another student taped that session of the seminar, and I asked if I might listen to his tape. Just between you and me, I wanted to revel a bit more in my academic victory. But my response to what I heard on the tape was anything but reveling. Though my intellectual points were solid, I was horrified by my tone. I sounded conceited, overconfident, and utterly obnoxious. I was shocked and embarrassed.

Since that eye-opening moment some twenty years ago, I've been trying to lose my arrogant tone, not to mention my arrogant heart. Things are somewhat better now, but, as the saying goes, God isn't finished with me yet. Just ask my family or my partners in church leadership. I remember a particularly tense moment in a meeting with the elders of my church. One elder shared what he thought was a fine idea, but for some reason, my anger spiked. I came after him with a flood of objections, including such helpful lines as "We'll do that over my dead body." It wasn't my most glorious moment. Thank God this elder was mature enough not to respond in kind.

Even if I had been one hundred percent right in my opinions, either in my graduate seminar or in the elder meeting, there was no defense for my mode of communication. Lying is sinful, of course. But so is truthful speech when it comes packaged in bluster and boastfulness. Far worse is telling the truth with meanness for the purpose of mowing people down. Divine truth, especially, must be spoken in a divinely prescribed manner. With all due respect to Teddy

Roosevelt, we should not wield a big stick in our efforts to be truthful. Rather, we must speak gently and bury our big stick. This is the clarion call of Scripture. It's a call that many of us need to take to heart.

God's Call to Gentleness and Humility

The Old Testament repeatedly commends humility. According to Psalm 25, the Lord "leads the humble in what is right, teaching them his way" (verse 9). The book of Proverbs agrees: "It is better to live humbly with the poor than to share plunder with the proud" (16:19). The fact that God prizes humility is seen in his choice of Moses, who "was more humble than any other person on earth" (Numbers 12:3). Even the long-awaited messianic King would come humbly to Jerusalem, according to the prophet Zechariah: "Rejoice greatly, O people of Zion! Shout in triumph, O people of Jerusalem! Look, your king is coming to you. He is righteous and victorious, yet he is humble, riding on a donkey" (Zechariah 9:9).

If you were to read any of these Old Testament verses in the ancient Greek translation, you'd find the word *praus* (or a derivation of this adjective). This word, which appears throughout the New Testament, means "humble" when it describes a person's attitude. When applied to behavior or speech, it means "gentle." For example, Jesus said that "the whole earth will belong" to those who are *praus,* humble in heart or gentle in action (Matthew 5:5). He also described himself this way: "Let me teach you, because I am humble *[praus]* and gentle, and you will find rest for your souls" (Matthew 11:29). According to Paul, all of us must clothe ourselves with this quality. It is one essential slice of the fruit of the Spirit.[1] When we are humble in heart, we will avoid treating people harshly, preferring instead to relate to them with gentleness that flows from humility.

The biblical call to humility and gentleness applies to a broad range of behavior, including the way we speak the truth. Several New Testament texts make this connection explicit. To these we will turn in a few moments. But before examining them we must be clear about what gentleness is not.

Don't Misread Gentleness

Gentleness is not wimpishness. A person who is gentle has plenty of strength but chooses not to summon it in deference to what will be more beneficial to others. When my son, Nathan, was a preschooler, he loved to wrestle with me. He almost always won our matches not because I was weak, but because I chose to be gentle rather than use my physical power. When a person speaks gently, it's not a sign of weakness, but rather of superior strength. Only those who have confidence in the truth of their message will speak gently, realizing that truth doesn't need overpowering volume to prevail. Truth possesses its own power.

Neither is gentleness an act of feigning weakness in order to manipulate others. It's nothing like the smarminess of Charles Dickens's classic character Uriah Heep, who uses his "'umbleness" as a way to gain power over the people around him. Heep pretends to be humble in speech and demeanor, yet all the while abusing the trust others have put in him so he can use them in his selfish schemes.[2] True gentleness comes from a desire to serve, not to dominate. It's not a rhetorical technique, but a sincere expression of one's humble heart.

Gentleness is also not fearful hesitancy. If you're feeling insecure about what to say, you might speak quietly, but this isn't gentleness so much as it is faint-heartedness. Gentle speech sometimes requires tremendous courage.

In 1994 Mother Teresa of Calcutta gave the keynote address at the National Prayer Breakfast in Washington, D.C. This diminutive, physically un-impressive woman spoke to a room of four thousand, including President and Mrs. Clinton, Vice President and Mrs. Gore, and a host of other national leaders. She wasn't a spellbinder, at least not as a public speaker. A model of gentleness, she spoke clearly but quietly, focusing her early remarks on the love of God and the promise of peace.

But then her message took a shocking turn. In front of some of the most powerful people in the world, many of whom were staunch supporters of abortion rights, she began to speak of her commitment to life for unborn children. Not mincing her words, she said, "Any country that accepts abortion is not teaching its people to love, but to use any violence to get what they want. This is why the greatest destroyer of love and peace is abortion."[3] When making this bold declaration, Mother Teresa did not raise her voice or criticize any person by name. Her tone was gentle, her demeanor humble. Her intention was not to disgrace those who disagreed with her, but to change their hearts. She spoke the truth as she perceived it, confident not in her powers of persuasion, but in the power of the truth.[4]

Whether or not we agree with Mother Teresa's view, her example of gentleness is instructive to all of us. When the Bible calls us to gentleness, it does not commend weakness, obsequiousness, or hesitancy of speech. Rather, it endorses speaking the truth with quiet confidence, avoiding severity or harshness. When we know we're on the side of truth, not to mention on the side of the God of truth, then we can speak with genuine humility and kindness, even when the stakes are high.

The Power of Gentleness

Having noted that the Bible commends gentleness but not weakness, let us now consider three situations where the New Testament specifically advises us to be gentle when speaking the truth.

1. Speak Gently in the Face of Accusation

Early Christians were frequently the target of criticism. In the latter half of the first century A.D., believers living in what is now northern Turkey were being attacked for their faith. The apostle Peter wrote a letter to these suffering Christians to encourage them to be steadfast.

"If you are asked about your Christian hope," Peter said, "always be ready to explain it" (1 Peter 3:15). In context, it's clear that those asking about Christian faith were not doing so out of genuine interest. The questions were part of an attack being waged upon believers by pagans who resented the counter-cultural commitments of the Christians. Loyalty to Christ had replaced former loyalties to family, work, city, and even the Roman Empire itself. This angered some people who sought to make the Christians pay for their "superstitious" and "antisocial" faith in Christ.

In light of this challenge, Peter called for a rational, courtroom-type response. "Offer a *defense* by giving your accusers the *reason* for your hope," he urged (see 1 Peter 3:15). And with what tone? Never with boastful defensiveness or a hard-hitting accusation. Peter continued, "But you must do this in a gentle and respectful way" (1 Peter 3:16). Even those who are making false accusations deserve a measured, kind response. Why? "Then if people speak evil against you," Peter explained, "they will be ashamed when they see what a good life you live because you belong to Christ" (verse 16). If the Christians defended themselves with harshness, their tone would only serve to confirm the accusations against them. In contrast, their gentleness would render the allegations impotent. Moreover, by returning kindness for cruelty, the believers were imitating Jesus' own response to suffering and thereby presenting an incredibly powerful witness for the Lord.[5]

During my college years I witnessed an excellent example of this Christlike gentleness. Os Guinness was delivering a number of well-attended public lectures on the Christian faith at Yale University. The crowd, comprising both Christians and non-Christians, responded to Os with respect whether or not they agreed with his views. Except for one man. At the close of the first lecture, the man stood up and made a short speech that attacked Os and his ideas. The speaker's words and tone were rude. When he finally finished, all eyes turned to Os. I was ready for him to skewer this man with his incisive intellect. But, to my surprise, Os began by finding something in the man's speech with which he agreed. Then on the basis of this common ground, Os carefully explained the differences between them. He was calm and not at all defensive. His kindness toward his assailant was so undeserved and gracious that it impressed us all. I'm quite sure Os's demeanor encouraged unbelievers in the audience to listen even more sympathetically to his lectures. I determined that Friday evening that I would try to be like Os.

Why did Os Guinness explain the hope within him in such a gentle and respectful way? I'm sure he did this in part out of his commitment to obey the Scriptures.[6] I expect he also knew that a gentle response would win the audience's favor, regardless of its impact on the angry man. But, more than this, Os was confident in the truth. He knew that divine truth didn't warrant a tirade. If anything, the quietness of his response accentuated the power of the truth he uttered.

2. Speak Gently in Personal Confrontation

Suppose you discover that a Christian brother or sister has been caught up in sin and has not yet reached the point of confessing or repenting. What should you do? Most people I know would say, "It's none of my business. It's between the individual and God."

In his letter to the Galatians, Paul dealt with this type of situation, one that is common in the life of the church. But his answer reflects his first-century understanding of Christian fellowship rather than the individualistic bias of American culture. He wrote, "Dear brothers and sisters, if another Christian is overcome by some sin, you who are godly should gently and humbly help that person back onto the right path. And be careful not to fall into the same temptation yourself" (6:1). Your job, Paul explained, is to get involved, to help the person overcome sin and find release from bondage.

Notice carefully what this text advocates. We should "help that person back onto the right path." The original language used in this sentence employs a verb that means "to restore" or "to mend." It describes, for example, what fishermen do when they fix their torn nets. Although the process of mending a person caught in sin will require confrontation, perhaps even unwelcome accusation, the purpose is to restore that individual. If this is going to happen, harshness must be completely ruled out. Rather, Paul advised, "you who are godly should gently and humbly help that person." Only this tone of communication has a chance of reaching the heart of the sinning brother or sister.

Early in my tenure at Irvine Presbyterian Church, a member who was unhappy with my leadership sent me a scorching letter. It seemed to burn my hands as well as my heart. John criticized my preaching, my leadership, you name it. But he went beyond my actions to attack my intentions and character. He accused me of using his church merely as a stepping stone for my own professional advancement. In John's mind, I would remain at Irvine for a couple of years, only until a more impressive church sought my pastoral services. He alleged that I was overcome with the sins of self-centeredness, dishonesty, and pride.

There might have been grains of truth in his tirade, but I couldn't receive any part of it. I felt hurt, angry, defensive. An emotional Great Wall of China separated me from my brother in Christ. It took several days of cooling off, along with lots of prayer and support from others, before I was ready to respond. When I finally sat down with John to talk, it was still very hard for me to hear what he was really trying to say.

Of course I needed to tell John how his letter had affected me and confront him with his inconsiderate language. By God's grace and because I had practiced my speech dozens of times, I was able to speak honestly and kindly. I was amazed when he could actually hear me. He admitted that his letter had been far too abrasive and that he should not have attacked my character. At the end of our meeting, we prayed together and promised to work hard on our relationship.

I'm sorry to say that this episode with John was not the last. During the next several years, I received a few more letters like the first one, though the tone slowly improved. We'd get together and hash out both the substance of his concern and the unhelpfulness of his communication style. In time he learned that he didn't have to accuse me of sinning to get my attention, and I learned to listen to his heart even when his words offended me. Eventually John stopped attacking me. If something I did worried him, he'd shoot me a quick note, addressing the behavior but not assaulting my heart. By the time John moved to another city much later, he and I had established an open, trusting relationship.

I apologize if this story seems a bit self-serving. There have been many times when I have been correctly and appropriately confronted not only for mistakes in leadership, but for sin, plain and simple. For instance, some time ago a man made an appointment to see me. Jordan said he needed to share something that was hard to talk about. Thinking he was going to talk about something difficult in his life, I invited him to continue. But the difficult subject was not his shortcoming, it was *mine*.

During the weeks prior to our meeting, Jordan's former wife had been calling the church, wanting to speak to the pastor. Although she and Jordan had been divorced for several years, she was still furious with him. She wanted me to know about his failures. I listened to this woman and tried to appease her. My efforts failed, however, because when she didn't get the satisfaction she sought from me, she called other members of my staff. Finally, I talked with her again and told her not to call our church anymore. I thought the matter was finished. Throughout this time I never called Jordan to tell him what was going on. I guess I wanted to spare him even more misery. But he ended up hearing about it from several sources and was angry that I didn't have the decency to call him. He told me this bluntly but humbly. He didn't attack my character, but he did say that he thought I had done wrong in my failure to talk directly with him.

As he spoke, I felt my pulse quicken and my heart begin to take a defensive posture. But Jordan's gentleness kept me from putting my guard up completely. I realized that he was right, that I had wronged him by talking behind his back without speaking directly to him. I apologized and asked his forgiveness, which he freely gave. Our reconciliation was both quick and lasting, owing to Jordan's ability to do what Paul commended in Galatians 6 by gently and humbly helping me get back on the right track.

Of course it's no fun being the giver *or* the receiver in these situations. But if we are truly members of one another in Christ's body, then we'll work on speaking and hearing difficult truth with gentleness, so that we might grow together in Christ.

3. Speak Gently When Refuting Theological Error

It's one thing to hear theological falsehoods from unbelievers. What else should we expect? But when fellow Christians deny fundamental tenets of the faith, this really gets my goat. Some members of my own denomination, for example, have publicly questioned the lordship of Christ and the authority of Scripture. My first reaction, I must admit, is to want to bop them on the head—metaphorically speaking. I want to take them on, to put them in their place.

But the very Scripture I am so eager to defend says, "No bopping allowed."

In his second letter to Timothy, the apostle Paul helped his disciple deal with Christians who denied fundamental theological truths. "The Lord's servants must not quarrel," Paul said, "but must be kind to everyone" (2:24)—not just to those with whom we agree theologically, but to *everyone*. This includes people whose basic theology is wrong. According to Paul, we should "gently teach those who oppose the truth" (2:25). Notice, no arguing, no putting our theological opponents in their place. Rather, we are to be gentle, especially with those who oppose the truth. Why is this tone of communication necessary? Paul explained, "Perhaps God will change those people's hearts, and they will believe the truth" (2:25). If we who claim to be orthodox hammer away on the heretics, they'll scarcely be drawn to the truth. But if we treat them in a way that mirrors the gospel we seek to defend, their minds and hearts may well be transformed.

Thinking back to my obnoxious behavior in my graduate seminar, I realize that I reacted so harshly against my fellow student not because I disliked his academic work but because I disagreed with his religious beliefs. He was a member of the Unification Church, a follower of the Reverend Sun Myung Moon, one of the most notorious cult leaders in the world. Among Reverend Moon's heretical views, he considered himself to be the second coming of Christ. My fellow student saw himself as not only a Christian, but a super-Christian, one who had transcended my old-fashioned Christianity with a better, Moon-centered version. This bugged me big time. The seminar gave me a chance not merely to win academic points, but to vanquish my theological opponent. In my vanquishing, however, I did not move him any closer to embracing the truth about Jesus. If anything, my roughness pushed him farther from it.

But intellectual debate and godly gentleness are not mutually exclusive. I have seen Christians meld superior intelligence with superior humility when responding to people who espouse heretical ideas. For example, Dallas Willard is one of the most brilliant people I know. A full professor of philosophy at the University of Southern California, he comprehends contemporary philosophy like no one else. As a Christian, he has applied his mind to understanding God's revelation in Scripture. His outstanding writings demonstrate his success in this endeavor. If anyone could claim mastery of the truth, if anyone might be allowed a bit of arrogance, it would be Dallas Willard. But no allowance is needed.

Years ago I invited Dallas to teach an adult class at my church. During each session in the twelve-week term, he spent about forty minutes lecturing and twenty minutes in dialogue with class members. Some of the comments from the students were not just slightly off base, but simply wrong. More than once I heard folks from my church argue points that were obviously heretical. Yet Dallas never addressed with disrespect the people who said such things. With exceptional humility and exceptional insight, he spoke of the truth he had found in God's Word, correcting people where correction was needed, but never making them feel small.

Don't you long to be like Dallas Willard, one who knows God's truth yet communicates it gently? If we imitate his example, people will gladly listen to us, even if they don't share our convictions. We'll build bridges rather than walls. But this is much easier said than done.

One Good Friday afternoon, I had an opportunity to imitate Dallas Willard's graciousness while participating in a radio talk-show discussion. The talk-show host, Hugh Hewitt, had invited me to come on his program to discuss the meaning of the cross of Christ with two women who vehemently denied its goodness. They had written a book in which they argued that the Cross was nothing more than a violent, tragic event. Christian theology, they wrote, enthrones child abuse by picturing the heavenly Father sending his Son to die on a cross.

With grave trepidation, I accepted Hugh's invitation to debate these two women. My reticence didn't have to do with any insecurity about my ability to defend Christian orthodoxy. But it had everything to do with my own visceral reaction to the views of these two women. I felt angry and incensed by their positions. The fact that they claimed to be Christians bugged me even more. A substantial part of me wanted to do some serious bopping.

But I knew better. I believed that God had given me this opportunity not to devastate my opponents, but to speak plainly of the true meaning of the Cross and to speak gently because that's what the Cross commends.

After the show was over, people who listened told me that I did well, both in content and in tone. If this is true, God gets all the credit. I spent hours in the days before that program praying for a truly humble spirit and for the ability to tell the truth with gentleness. I asked dozens of Christian friends to hold me up in prayer. I believe that the Lord answered our prayers, allowing me to be far more gentle than I would have been if left to my own devices.

Is There Ever an Occasion for Yelling?

Given all that I have been saying about gentle communication, you might wonder if there's ever an occasion in which it's right to raise our voices. If we look to Scripture, we find that shouting is appropriate at times. The crowds hollered "Hosanna!" when Jesus entered Jerusalem on Palm Sunday. Jesus himself shouted on a few occasions, such as when he ordered Lazarus to come out of the grave. The apostle Paul shouted at the Philippian jailer to keep him from hurting himself. But on none of these occasions were voices raised for the purpose of getting the truth across.

Though we might rightly shout if a person is in danger or if the noisiness of a certain environment prevents quiet conversation, Scripture provides little support for the appropriateness of raising our voices, especially when it's combined with harshness. Of course, the cruelest words can sometimes be spoken quietly. The real issue isn't so much volume as it is tone and intention.

I am concerned, however, about the tendency of people to raise their voices in anger, often joining volume with malice. I watch drivers scream at the "idiot" in front of them or parents cuss out the "stupid" umpire at a Little League game. I hear spouses cut each other down when they come to me for counseling. Some of them still uphold the damaging ideology popularized in the sixties and seventies: "Ya gotta let it all hang out. Ya gotta be real." According to this destructive view, being real means discharging anger as if from a shotgun. If it blows someone else away, it's the victim's fault for being too weak to handle reality. In the guise of honesty, husbands and wives cut each other down without mercy, often damaging their marriages beyond repair.

I reject that self-centered ideology completely, both because it is inconsistent with Scripture and because it just doesn't work. Yet you wouldn't always be able to tell by listening to me. I sometimes blast away at the ones I love the most. My wife gets a good bellow from me every now and then. My children get more than an occasional yell. I find it far too easy to raise my voice, not just when I'm cheering for them in soccer or warning them about danger, but when I'm trying to get them to grasp the truth, or at least what I think is the truth.

I'm not suggesting that every increase of volume is always wrong. If you're a parent, you'll need to consider your behavior in light of God's Word. But I'll confess that I yell too meanly and too much. I can hurt my children's feelings unnecessarily. I can make them feel ashamed. And I know I'm not the only parent who does this.

I bring up this issue not because it's my "stuff," but because I'm deeply concerned about how we can injure our loved ones through harsh communication, whether loud or quiet. With our words and even our silence we can injure their spirits. Sometimes we defend our behavior on the grounds that we have to get our spouses or our children to acknowledge the truth. The goal is worthy, but the methods are not. The Bible exhorts fathers, "Don't make your children angry by the way you treat them" (Ephesians 6:4). It also says, "Fathers, don't aggravate your children. If you do, they will become discouraged and quit trying" (Colossians 3:21). When this happens, some of us just yell louder, creating more aggravation, more discouragement, and more quitting.

It's not easy for me to write about this because it is a current struggle for me. I feel pretty vulnerable and ashamed, to tell you the truth. But I am hoping that my candor will encourage you to look closely at your own life. Maybe you are never harsh with your children or your spouse, or with your employees or your colleagues. If not, thanks be to God. But if, like me, you realize that your behavior falls short of divine standards, then I'd invite you to join me in confessing your sin to the Lord and seeking the help of his Spirit. I know that God can change even deeply ingrained habits if we offer ourselves to him humbly and truly.

A FOUNDATION OF GENTLE TRUTHFULNESS

Earlier in this chapter we noted Peter's advice to explain the hope within us "in a gentle and respectful way" (1 Peter 3:16). The wording of this English translation makes it hard to see exactly what Peter was saying. Literally, the verse calls us to defend our faith "with gentleness and reverent fear." In this verse, gentleness is directed toward those who receive the defense, but reverent fear goes upward, so to speak. We must be gentle with others and reverent before God.

Why did Peter mention reverence? What is the relationship between speaking the truth gently and fearing the Lord? Humility is the virtue that links the two. When we consider the greatness and holiness of God, our hearts are filled not only with reverence but also with humility. With this attitude we will speak of our faith neither arrogantly nor harshly, but with gentleness. When we're on our knees before the one and only Master of the truth, we won't be able to pretend that *we* are masters of the truth. Thus, our gentleness is both an imitation of Christ and a result of humbly venerating his greatness.

We find a stirring example of this kind of reverent humility in Abraham Lincoln's Second Inaugural Address. As the Civil War drew to a close early in 1865, the North was poised to defeat the South after years of agonizing bloodshed. Many Northern voices called for Southerners to be punished for their crimes against the Union. Understandably, they expected Lincoln to fill his Second Inaugural with praises of his own military success and promises of retribution against the South. But the president confounded these expectations. In a political speech that sounded more like a sermon, Lincoln meditated upon the awesome sovereignty and justice of God. So humbled before the "Living God," Lincoln argued that the victorious North ought to act not with arrogant vengefulness, but "with malice toward none; with charity for all; with firmness in the right, as God gives us to see the right."[7] Thus, as Ronald C. White Jr. concludes in his book *Lincoln's Greatest Speech,* "Neither vindication nor triumphalism is present in the Second Inaugural. At the bedrock is Lincoln's humility."[8] This humility, as White aptly demonstrates, stemmed from the president's vision of God's transcendent justice and power. Thus, he delivered his Second Inaugural

Address not with arrogance or animosity, but with reverence and gentleness, as a man humbled before the living God.

The stirring example of Abraham Lincoln reminds us that if we wish to speak more kindly, we mustn't merely try changing our words. It isn't even enough to try to have a humble heart, though this is essential. True gentleness and humility come through our relationship with God. So, in addition to striving for gentleness and humility, seek first the presence of God in your life, and these other things will be yours as well.

TRUTH IN THE TRENCHES

TELLING THE TRUTH WHEN IT'S TRICKY

Throughout this book I have readily acknowledged that it can be difficult to tell the truth. But at times, "difficult" doesn't begin to tell the story. In some situations complete honesty is downright excruciating.

I asked members of my weekly Bible study group to tell me when they found it most difficult to be truthful. One woman shared that she had been the "perfect" daughter in her family and had always pleased her parents. When her husband's unfaithfulness ruined her marriage, she dreaded telling her parents what had happened, knowing how disappointed they would be. A man told a similar story, remembering how hard it was to tell his children that he and their mother were getting a divorce. In both of these situations, the speakers dreaded the pain that the truth would inflict upon the recipients and, ultimately, upon themselves.

One of my most excruciating struggles with truthfulness happened a few years ago when my church called a new associate pastor named Kirk. Because housing costs so much in our community, Kirk and his wife, Emily, had a terrible time finding a comfortable yet affordable house. Even with a substantial loan from the church, their search was a nightmare. Finally, after a yearlong effort, they found a cozy home not too far from our church.

Arranging the financing wasn't much easier than finding the house itself. Most lending institutions don't like to mess with churches or with housing loans for pastors because, I've been told, they fear the negative press that would come if they had to foreclose. But finally, Kirk found a mortgage broker who agreed to arrange a loan. The timing was tight, however. All the pieces had to come together in just the right order or Kirk and Emily would lose both their house and their substantial deposit.

A few days before the closing, I received a call from Kirk's broker. "I've got a few forms for you to sign on behalf of the church," he said. "Nothing tricky."

"No problem," I answered. "Just send them my way and I'll sign."

"There is one little thing, however," he added. "One of the forms asks you to state that the church doesn't expect Kirk and Emily to repay the loan you're giving them."

"But that isn't what we're doing," I objected. "I don't know how I could sign that form."

"I know, but it's no big deal. People do this all the time. I know what the church is doing, and so does the lending institution. They just don't want it in writing."

"I don't think I can sign," I protested.

"Look," the broker continued. "I'll send over the form. You'll see that it's a no-brainer. Don't worry."

"And if I don't sign?" I queried.

"Well, then the loan won't be funded, and the deal will fall through. Surely you don't want that!"

No, indeed I did not. A few minutes later the form was faxed to my office. I desperately hoped that somehow it was worded in a way that would give me an out. But the wording was all too clear. I was supposed to sign a statement alleging that our church was giving Kirk money for the house with no expectation of repayment. This simply wasn't the case.

As I sat at my desk, my heart felt heavier than a bowling ball. If I stood for the truth, then Kirk and Emily would lose their home plus thousands of dollars they had already paid up-front. They'd be devastated, and the church would be disappointed. If, on the other hand, I signed the form, then the sale would go through, Kirk and Emily would move into their home, and nobody would ever know what I did, except the broker who was urging me to do it. That would be the end of it, if I could find a way to squelch my hyperactive conscience.

No one will be hurt by a fib that everybody tells all the time anyway, I told myself. *No one will care. Everyone will benefit. Yes, I'll feel guilty, but that will pass.* Yet how could I do what I knew to be wrong? Conversely, how could I, because of my inflexibility, hurt so many people I cared for? With an anguished soul I called out to God: "Lord, what should I do now?" The cost of my truthfulness could be the loss of another couple's home. It seemed too high a price to pay.

THE HIGH COST OF TRUTH

Why can it be so hard to tell the truth? The various answers to this question generally fall under three headings: *content, context,* and *consequences.*

The Challenge of Content

Sometimes we struggle to tell the truth because we're not sure what the truth actually is. This happens when the situations we seek to address are complex and confusing. For example, a man came to me because his marriage was on the rocks. "Can you tell me what's wrong?" I asked. He sat quietly for several seconds before answering, "I'm not exactly sure what to say." As we began to talk, I understood his confusion. The issues in his marriage were convoluted and difficult to fathom. He wanted to tell the truth, but he struggled at the challenge because he just wasn't sure what the truth was.

The Challenge of Context

Even if we're pretty sure about the content of the truth, the context of communication can make truth speaking tricky. For instance, if you're in a relationship that has been characterized by deception in the past, changing course midstream won't be easy. When one child in a family finally sees the truth that Mom is an alcoholic, sharing this with other family members can take a tremendous amount of courage. Truth is harder to deliver when it is preceded by weeks, or even years, of deception.

Our work environment also can hinder our commitment to truthfulness. If your boss expects you to support her vision no matter what you actually think, you'll feel strong pressure to keep your true thoughts to yourself. Or perhaps you work in a company pervaded by deceit. Today's headlines testify to the power of corporate deception to suck otherwise honest people into its muck.

In the gospel of Matthew, Jesus addressed another challenging context for telling the truth. What should you do if someone in the church sins against you? Ignore the offense? Leave the church? Defend yourself to your friends? Gossip about the offending party? Confront the offender directly? It's easy to recognize the last option as the right answer, but it's much harder to carry out Jesus' clear directive and speak the truth in such an awkward situation.

The Challenge of Consequences

By far, the greatest inhibitor to complete honesty is the fear of consequences. When we believe that the truth can hurt people, we refrain from forthrightness, often choosing a so-called white lie instead.

One day, a heavy-hearted thirty-five-year-old single man named Dennis came to see me. "Women just don't seem to like me," he lamented, "and I don't know why they don't want to go out with me. The few who do agree to a date don't want to be in a serious relationship. Pastor, do you know why women don't like me?"

In truth, I had a pretty good idea. He was one of the most egotistical people I knew. He was his own favorite subject, hobby, and not-so-secret admirer. He rarely asked questions about others, and when he did, he listened poorly, waiting to jump back in with more information about himself. Though I'm no expert on women, most women I know are looking for a companion who cares about something other than himself.

As I considered my response, I dreaded being honest. The truth would be hard for Dennis to hear. Moreover, I knew that his social dysfunction came from his own wounded spirit. If I were to say, "The reason women don't like you is that you talk about yourself too much," I might well have wounded him further. I knew it was my job as this man's pastor to tell him the truth, but I feared the consequences: more hurt and perhaps even anger at me. How much easier it would have been to say, "Ah, c'mon, Dennis. You just haven't found the right woman yet. Don't worry about it. Surely all women don't dislike you. You've just had a run of bad luck."

After thinking about my options and praying silently for God's help, I decided to be truthful in the most gentle way I could imagine. "I'm not sure why women don't seem to like you, Dennis," I began. "But tell me, what do you think women want most in a man?" It took awhile, but eventually I helped him "discover" that women like men who truly care about their feelings and who demonstrate this care by listening. At this point I asked, "So how are you at listening to women?" He admitted that he didn't do this very well. From that point we were able to talk about what kept Dennis from listening (insecurity) and how he might become a better listener (lots of prayer and practice).

Like most people, I also struggle with truthfulness when the consequences hurt me. I face this challenge every year at tax time. In addition to my pastoral salary, I receive a fair amount of income that doesn't get reported directly to the IRS (for example, my parsonage allowance or honoraria for speaking engagements). Though my church, publishers, and seminaries report my income to the IRS, a portion of what I receive is unreported unless I do it. Legally and morally I'm required to declare this income. But it's hard to do when I know it will cost me a few thousand dollars in additional taxes—money I would be able to keep if I simply didn't report my excess income. The consequence of honesty in this situation is costly in a literal sense, and that makes it hard to tell the truth.

HELP IN THE TRENCHES

Given the challenges of content, context, and consequences, it can be agonizing to tell the truth. What, then, will help us rise to the challenge? What will encourage us to tell the truth in the trenches of life when it is complicated and costly?

If you'll forgive my preacher's love for alliteration, I'd like to suggest five avenues of encouragement, all of which start with the letter *c*. In the tough situations of life, we'll be helped by the *commandment* of God, our *commitment* to truthfulness, the *counsel* of Scripture, the *Counselor* who teaches us, and the *community* of Christ.

The Commandment of God

In previous chapters we've seen that the Bible calls us to a life of complete honesty. The ninth commandment prohibits false testimony. The Psalms and the New Testament agree that God's people should reject falsehood in favor of the truth. Moreover, the nature of God as the Truthful Trinity seals the case for honesty. As people created in God's image and set apart to be like him, we should speak and live out the truth. Hence, the biblical commandment against lying.

But must we *always* obey this commandment? Must we *always* tell the truth? Aren't there some cases in which it's morally permissible to lie?

Consider, for example, a situation where the issues are relatively trivial and where a "little white lie" appears to make everybody feel better. A recent column in *Newsweek* addressed the ordeal of vacationing with family and offered several ways to reduce stress, including some advice on lying:

> Of course, you can never tell your family that they're driving you crazy. But a white lie won't hurt. Need some free time? Say your doctors insist you take hour long walks each day. "There's nothing wrong with a lie," [psychologist Jason] Kornrich says. "As long as it sounds convincing."[1]

What harm would there be in telling a little white lie to preserve family harmony? Surely it's no big deal, no serious sin.

You'll search in vain for the biblical passages that excuse lying in such situations. Scripture nowhere says, "Tell your neighbor the truth, except when it's no big deal." Furthermore, the whole rationale behind lying for convenience falls apart when considered from the perspective of the recipient. According to Sissela Bok in her classic study of lying, "Liars share with those they deceive the desire not to *be* deceived."[2] When people argue for the rightness of "little white lies," they rarely think in terms of the Golden Rule, treating others the same way they want to be treated. Instead, they focus on their own comfort and convenience. A white lie is usually convenient for one person only: the person who is telling it.

Those who condone the white lie are overlooking the complex interconnectedness of human life. If we take the short-term view when lying to a relative about needing to take a walk and saying that it needs to be an hour-long walk that is taken *alone*, then a little deception seems to be harmless. But what if we do this sort of thing not just once, but repeatedly, as is usually the case with people who excuse "minor" deceptions? What will happen in the heart of the little white liar? I would suggest that this person's heart will slowly become blackened with the soot of deceit. Habitual lying about small things prepares us to deliver increasingly significant distortions. Thus, a president who once fibbed about relatively minor details of his background in graduate school ends up lying even when under oath during an official inquiry. According to ethicist Michael Josephson, "Lies are like potato chips. You can't tell just one."[3] If I can't speak plainly to my family ("I love you dearly, but I really need some time to myself. I'm going for a walk, and I'll be back in about an hour"), then I will be totally unprepared to tell the truth when the stakes are a lot higher.

Moreover, think about what happens in a family when members can't be honest with one another about their needs. Superficial conflicts may be avoided, but at a cost far greater than the white liar realizes. What is lost in the transaction is an authentic, growing, healthy relationship. With the lie, you lose the ability to be yourself with your own family. To be sure, the moment one says, "I need to take a walk right now because I just need some time alone" may be uncomfortable. But it can lead to healthy, open conversation about family dynamics and personal needs. After all, truth is all about honesty and openness.

What about lying in situations where the stakes are far higher than family harmony during vacation? The classic case comes from the era of the Nazi domination of Europe. Many Christians who risked their lives by hiding Jews were asked directly by Gestapo officers if they were harboring Jews. An honest answer would have led to the death of the hidden Jews and the truthful Christian as well. Surely, many argue, in such a case lying is the best option and not a sin.

A situation such as this impales us on the horns of an ethical dilemma. Either you lie or you are an accessory to murder. There is no middle ground. Lying *may* in this case be the lesser of two evils. Thus, in the Old Testament when Rahab lied to protect the lives of the Jewish spies, God rewarded her without condemning her for her dishonesty. Some theologians argue that if Rahab had told the truth, God would nevertheless have spared both her and the spies. Scripture nowhere teaches this, however, even if it's true. Moreover, in the New Testament Rahab exemplifies both faith and good works (see Hebrews 11:31 and James 2:25).

But *if* it is morally permissible to lie in a situation when telling the truth would lead directly to some dire consequence, we must admit the rarity of such circumstances. Throughout my life I have repeatedly heard people excuse lying. *Not once* has the issue been a matter of life and death. The question What should the Christians have said to the Nazis? serves mainly to justify lying in far less critical situations. Furthermore, if we excuse lying when life really hangs in the balance, we must beware of our tendency to slide down the slippery slope of rationalization. At the top of this slope, we begin by allowing deception when it protects human life. At the bottom we end up defending white lies because we want to escape from annoying relatives on a family vacation.

The commandment of God to live in complete honesty should guide our behavior in every area of life. If there are exceptions, these are so rare as to be virtually irrelevant for most of us in the Western world.

Our Commitment to Truthfulness

If we take Scripture seriously, we'll make a bedrock commitment to truthfulness. Like a witness in court, we will swear to tell the truth, the whole truth, and nothing but the truth, so help us God. Though we may struggle at times to determine the precise nature of the truth, and though the consequences of honesty may be daunting, we will seek to be truthful no matter what.

In an earlier chapter we saw that a commitment to avoiding deception is an essential precursor to truthful living. Now we must take a further step by making a commitment to truthfulness. A commitment is more than an imprecise inclination. It is an explicit statement of intention, a vow that will govern future decisions and behavior. It's saying more than, "Well, I'll *try* to tell the truth." It's a promise made in the presence of God as well as those who can hold you accountable: "With your help, Lord, I *will* be truthful."

God does help us live up to this commitment in many and various ways. Yet he is honored not only when we fulfill our commitment to truthfulness, but even in the commitment itself. God delights in the fact that we take him seriously enough to reject the moral compromises of our culture in favor of a commitment to holy truthfulness. Our promise to live truthfully becomes, in fact, an act of worship in which we bow before our sovereign, holy God.

The Counsel of Scripture

As we have noted, the Bible commands us not to lie, but to speak the truth. Scripture also offers specific guidance for how we can be truthful in sticky situations. I could point to many relevant passages, such as Jesus' teaching about what to do if a fellow believer sins against you (see Matthew 18:15-17) or James's advice about confessing our sins to one another (see James 5:16). But I want to focus on one crucial text from Ephesians, where our growth in Christ depends upon our "speaking the truth in love" (4:15, NIV).

This passage underscores the value of honesty. The church, the body of Christ, will only grow to maturity if we, the members of the body, speak the truth. But more is required than simply saying true things. The way we communicate these true things makes all the difference in the world. We must speak not just the truth, but the truth in love. And sometimes this means not speaking at all.

In the film *Liar, Liar,* Jim Carrey plays the role of Fletcher Reede, a lawyer who can't stop lying. His penchant for deception backfires when his five-year-old son, tired of his dad's fibs, makes a birthday wish that his dad won't be able to lie for one entire day. Magically, the wish comes true, and the formerly fraudulent Reede finds himself unable to say anything false. Of course, he can't control his tongue either. So he ends up saying things that get him into a heap of trouble. Some of his comments are also quite mean. When the receptionist in his office, who sports a bizarre hairstyle, asks, "Do you like my new dress?" Reede answers honestly, "Whatever takes the focus off your head!" And when an obese colleague says, "What's up, Fletcher?" he responds, "Your cholesterol, fatty." Now we can't impugn Fletcher's truthfulness, but his honesty falls far short of the biblical standard of speaking the truth *in love*.[4]

According to Ecclesiastes, there is "a time to be quiet and a time to speak up" (3:7). So it is when it comes to speaking honestly. Sometimes we have to say true things, hard things. But sometimes, out of love, we simply hold our tongue.

Several years ago, at my church's men's retreat, a brand-new believer named Daniel gave his testimony. Though there was no question about his genuine faith in Christ, Daniel's theology was shot through with heresy. Before becoming a Christian, he had been a member of a bizarre religious cult. And, though he had genuinely acknowledged Jesus as his Lord and Savior, Daniel's head was still full of lots of theological rubbish. As he spoke, I wondered what I should do. Should I publicly correct his errors, much to his embarrassment? Or should I remain quiet and risk an implicit endorsement of Daniel's unorthodox beliefs? What did it mean to speak the truth in love at that moment?

As I prayed for God's guidance, I realized that virtually all the men in the room also felt awkward. They knew that Daniel was speaking heresy. Their orthodoxy was certainly not in danger. So, out of love, I didn't correct Daniel on the spot. I knew there would be plenty of time for him to grow in the truth. When he finished speaking, I thanked him for his openness and commended his genuine faith in Christ. Apart from that, I kept quiet.

Now, years after that incident, Daniel is a mature Christian with a solidly orthodox faith. What has made the difference? Years of truth-speaking in love. Some of the men on the retreat invited Daniel to join their Bible study group. In this loving context they were able to expose Daniel to biblical truth and correct his errors in light of Scripture. They didn't batter him with their orthodox sledgehammers, but gently and lovingly helped him grow in the full knowledge of God.

God calls us to pervasive truthfulness. We are to be people who practice complete honesty. But this does not mean saying whatever comes into our heads. Our honesty must always be shaped with the call to love as well as by the Holy Spirit, our divine Counselor.

The Counselor Who Teaches Us

To help us speak honestly, God provides not only the counsel of Scripture but also the Counselor who is promised in Scripture. After warning his disciples that the world will hate them, Jesus said, "But I will send you the Counselor—the Spirit of truth. He will come to you from the Father and will tell you all about me" (John 15:26). Moreover, Jesus added, this Counselor, the Holy Spirit, will teach us "everything" (John 14:26). The Greek word translated "counselor" also means "comforter, encourager, advocate." The Spirit of God plays all of these roles in our lives.

The Spirit as Counselor helps us speak truth in challenging situations. Jesus anticipated one of these situations when he said to his disciples,

> And when you are brought to trial in the synagogues and before rulers
> and authorities, don't worry about what to say in your defense, for the
> Holy Spirit will teach you what needs to be said even as you are standing
> there. (Luke 12:11-12)

It's hard to imagine a more stressful situation than this one, when saying the wrong thing—or the right thing!—could lead to severe punishment. Yet even in such a context we don't need to worry, Jesus says, because the Holy Spirit will help us say exactly the right thing.

Do you ask God to help you speak truthfully? I do, many times each week. Like the apostle Paul, I ask for "the right words" as I preach the gospel (Ephesians 6:19). I seek the Spirit's guidance for pastoral counseling, for leading staff meetings, and for disciplining my children. Over the years I have found that the Counselor does exactly what Jesus promised: He helps me speak truly even in difficult contexts.

The Community of Christ

In chapter 6 we saw that God places us in a community of like-minded believers so we can discern the truth and be encouraged to speak it. If we need the support of Christian brothers and sisters to live as truthful people each day, how much more do we require this help when the cost of truth is painfully high?

Earlier in this chapter I shared my yearly struggle with telling the truth at tax time. By God's grace I am not alone in facing this challenge. On the one hand, my wife, Linda, is exceptionally honest, and she would never support lying on our 1040 form. But if I somehow managed to evade Linda's scrutiny, I have yet another source of Christian accountability to keep me honest. My accountant, Bill, is a strong Christian with the highest ethical standards. I chose him to do my taxes in part because I was so impressed with his integrity. "You should pay every bit of tax that you legally owe," Bill explained in our first meeting, "but not a penny more." Because Bill knows the ins and outs of my professional life, he asks me to supply him with detailed information about areas where I might be most tempted to cheat. Though I don't enjoy the extra hours required to compile the data Bill demands, I am grateful for his commitment to help me be one hundred percent honest in all of my financial dealings.

As you consider your life, where are you most tempted to fudge the truth? In your business? With your friends? When you're applying for a job or trying to sell your used car? Who is there to help you be honest when you're tempted to lie? If you're trying to swim alone against the tide of deception in our world, you're underestimating the strength of the current. Let me urge you to share your struggle with a Christian brother or sister who can pray for you, encourage you, and hold you accountable when you most need it.

THE CONCERT OF ENCOURAGEMENT

Each of these avenues of encouragement—commandment, commitment, counsel, Counselor, community—helps us in the muddy trenches, in the raging battle between truth and falsehood. Taken together, they offer a concert of divine encouragement that inspires our truthfulness.

Remember my anguish over whether to sign the loan papers for my associate pastor's mortgage application? As the daunting form stared me in the face, I desperately needed all movements of this concert. I knew what Scripture commands, so the matter of right and wrong was never in question. But whether I'd choose to do right—or opt for wrong—was still in doubt.

The fact that I have made a commitment to tell the truth pushed me in the right direction. Although my track record is far from perfect, at least I have a history of intending to walk along the straight and narrow. If I had been in the habit of making false representations, I'm sure I would have found it much easier to do so in the case of Kirk's home loan paperwork.

Although the Bible doesn't provide specific guidance for filling out loan forms, it does repeatedly instruct us to share our struggles with our fellow believers. This is exactly what I needed. But whom should I call? As I prayed, a person came quickly to mind, no doubt with some help from the Counselor. Gary is an attorney by profession, an elder in the church, and a tender-hearted brother in Christ. It was way past time for me to share my burden with him.

As I reached Gary by phone, even the sound of his voice began to soothe my troubled heart. I was no longer alone in my struggle. I quickly explained the situation. I told him I knew that I shouldn't sign the loan form, but the thought of Kirk and Emily losing the house was keeping me from calling the broker and telling him my decision.

"You're absolutely right about that form," Gary began. "Don't sign it." If this was all Gary had said, it would have been enough. One tiny word of encouragement from a brother in Christ was all I needed to do the right thing.

Gary continued, "I don't know much about real estate law, but a friend of mine is an expert. Let me give him a call and find out about this loan situation. Then I'll call Kirk's broker and see what we can work out. There's got to be some way to solve this problem."

After thanking Gary for his help, I called Kirk to tell him I couldn't sign the form. He was surprisingly chipper, much more willing to trust God and even my judgment than I was. His support was a precious gift, and it also revealed a lot about Kirk's own commitment to honesty. Then I called his mortgage broker, whose predictably grumpy response reminded me of Eeyore on a bad day. He was sure that I had cost Kirk and his wife both their home and several thousand dollars.

If the story had ended there, it would serve as a painful reminder that truthfulness is sometimes costly. But the story didn't end there. I almost hesitate to relate the rest because I get tired of preachers whose examples promise rosy results when real life doesn't always work out that way. Truthfulness can lead to earthly blessing, but it sometimes leads to martyrdom. Jesus told the truth and look what happened to him. Nevertheless, I owe it to you to tell the whole story of what happened with Kirk's loan.

About three hours after I delivered the bad news to the mortgage broker, my assistant told me he was on the phone. "Great!" I thought. "Here we go again." I almost refused to take his call but figured I might as well get it over with.

"Hello, pastor," he began excitedly. "You won't believe what happened. I talked to your friend Gary and then I talked to the lending agency and told them what we were facing. They decided that if you sign a form stating that repayment of the church loan isn't due until Kirk sells the house, then they'll fund the loan after all."

"Now let me get this straight," I said incredulously. "I have to say that we expect the loan to be repaid, but only when Kirk's house is sold."

"Yes," the broker replied.

"But that's exactly the terms of our deal with Kirk. That's the truth."

"I know," the broker shouted. "You just have to tell the truth." I could sense from his excitement not only that he was glad the deal would go through but also that he was relieved we could be truthful. Though he hadn't let on before, he had been feeling uncomfortable about the lack of honesty in his former plan. But he had felt stuck, fearful that if he had insisted upon a truthful approach, he would have ruined the deal for Kirk and Emily.

So I signed a form that truthfully stated the nature of the church's loan to Kirk and Emily. And they got their house. And everyone lived happily ever after.

It's great when things work out this way. Someday, when the kingdom of this world has become the kingdom of our Lord and of his Christ, truth will finally and fully prevail. In the meantime, truthfulness sometimes leads to happy results, and sometimes it doesn't. But it's the best course, no matter what.

If my decision to tell the truth had led to Kirk and Emily's losing their home, I would have felt terrible about their loss. But I also would have known that I had made every effort to honor God. A clean conscience isn't anything to sneeze at. Besides, a dirty conscience often leads to messier encounters with sin. If I had lied about Kirk's loan, who knows if it would have been easier for me to lie the next time, and the next, and the next.

My experience with Kirk's loan led to many benefits aside from the most obvious one. If the ending of the loan story were not "happily ever after," I would still have known how God helps us be truthful even when the consequences seem gloomy. I would also have learned a badly needed lesson about relying on the body of Christ for support to live truthfully. And, even if Kirk had lost his home, he would have known how much his boss tries to be honest. If you've ever worked for a dishonest supervisor, you know how much truthfulness and trust matter. Even if my truthfulness had led to a mixed result, it would have led to many blessings.

TRUTH FOR THE BATTLE

Of course, had I known about these blessings in advance, my decision to tell the truth still wouldn't have been much easier, because I didn't want Kirk to lose his home. This side of heaven we don't automatically tell the truth with ease because we're engaged in a spiritual battle. As we read in Ephesians,

> Put on all of God's armor so that you will be able to stand firm against
> all strategies and tricks of the Devil. For we are not fighting against
> people made of flesh and blood, but against the evil rulers and authori-
> ties of the unseen world, against those mighty powers of darkness who

rule this world, and against wicked spirits in the heavenly realms.
(6:11-12)

If it feels as if you're living in the trenches in the midst of a great war, it's because you are.

Among the weapons employed by our chief opponent is deception. Even as the serpent deceived Adam and Eve, so the devil is "the one deceiving the whole world" (Revelation 12:9). "There is no truth in him," Jesus said, because "he is a liar and the father of lies" (John 8:44). Thus, in the midst of our spiritual battle, we should not be surprised to find ourselves shelled by falsehood and tempted to indulge in it. Likewise, we should not be surprised to discover that truth tops the list of the weapons God provides for our battle: "Use every piece of God's armor to resist the enemy in the time of evil, so that after the battle you will still be standing firm. Stand your ground, *putting on the sturdy belt of truth…*" (Ephesians 6:13-14). When we hold on to the truth even when it seems elusive, when we speak the truth even when it is costly, we will withstand the frontal assault of our spiritual enemy.

But truthfulness is more than hunkering down until the battle is over. It also is an offensive weapon through which we can successfully fight against the Enemy. According to Ephesians, after we put on our spiritual armor, we must "take the sword of the Spirit, which is the word of God" (6:17). With God's Word—God's revealed truth—we can cut through diabolical deception, because this Word is "full of living power" and "sharper than the sharpest knife" (Hebrews 4:12). The truth is one of God's mightiest weapons by which we can "knock down the Devil's strongholds" (2 Corinthians 10:4). The truth enables us to "break down every proud argument that keeps people from knowing God…conquer their rebellious ideas, and we teach them to obey Christ" (2 Corinthians 10:5). Thus, our truthfulness not only protects us in the trenches of life, but it also empowers us to draw others to Christ.

Aleksandr Solzhenitsyn was right. One word of truth does indeed outweigh the whole world. But the power of truth transcends this world. For this per-

spective we must look beyond the proverb of Solzhenitsyn to the poetry of
Martin Luther:

> And though this world, with devils filled, should threaten to undo us,
> We will not fear, for God hath willed His truth to triumph through us:
> The Prince of Darkness grim, We tremble not for him;
> His rage we can endure, For lo, his doom is sure;
> One little word shall fell him.

> That word above all earthly powers, No thanks to them, abideth;
> The Spirit and the gifts are ours Through Him who with us sideth:
> Let goods and kindred go, This mortal life also;
> The body they may kill: God's truth abideth still;
> His kingdom is forever. [5]

TRUTH WITH FEET

You Gotta Walk the Walk

What part of the body do you associate with truth? Perhaps you think of ears to hear the truth or eyes to see it. Or a nose to sniff out the truth. Maybe you link truth with the brain, the organ that helps us discern truth from falsehood. I expect that the majority of us would associate truth with the mouth because truth is something we speak.

Scripture makes this same association. The writer of Proverbs affirmed, "My mouth speaks what is true, for my lips detest wickedness" (8:7, NIV). Similarly, the psalmist prayed, "Do not snatch the word of truth from my mouth" (119:43, NIV). But often the Bible also connects truth with a different and unexpected part of the body. In Psalm 86 David prayed, "Teach me your way, O LORD, and I will walk in your truth" (verse 11, NIV). Correspondingly, John rejoiced because his spiritual children were "walking in the truth" (3 John 1:4, NIV). Truth, therefore, is a matter for the feet, not just the mouth. It has to do with the way we walk, not just how we speak. Truth and feet—a necessary but unforeseen association.

What Is "Walking in the Truth"?

The biblical writers spoke of *walking* where more literally minded folk would speak of *living*. Notice, for instance, how David phrased his commitment to moral integrity in Psalm 101: "I will walk in my house with blameless heart" (verse 2, NIV). He was obviously not talking about padding around the living room in his slippers. The *New Living Translation* renders the sense of this verse,

"I will lead a life of integrity in my own home." *To walk* means to live in a certain way. We use this same figure of speech when we say, "You gotta walk the walk if you're gonna talk the talk."

To walk *in truth,* therefore, is to live in accordance with the truth, whatever that might require of us. Shortly after my wedding, I believed the truth that Linda and I were married. If you had asked me, I would gladly have told you that we were husband and wife. But it took me quite some time before I consistently walked in the truth of my marital status. I was, for example, reluctant to surrender some of the freedom I had enjoyed as a single person. When Linda would ask me when I was coming home in the evening, I would balk, saying something vague like, "Well, I don't know yet because I'm not sure when I'll get done with work." Though I wanted to be married and I knew I was married, I wasn't yet *walking* in that truth. Now, some eighteen years later, I have learned to tell Linda when I'm planning to get home in the evening. Most of the time I even show up more or less when I'm due. In this small way and in countless others, I'm walking as a happily married man.

By loving my wife through the courtesy of telling her my daily schedule, I am walking in the biblical truth about marriage. I'm sharing life with Linda because she and I have become one flesh together. Walking in the truth of God isn't merely a matter of doing things we consider to be religious. It touches every facet of life. Our lives will be most meaningful and joyful when we walk in God's truth each day.

But how? What will help us walk in divine truth? Actually, the better question is not what but who. *Who* will help us walk in the truth? God will. In fact, as we learned in chapter 5, he is the world's most effective instructor in truthful living. Even as God trains us to speak the truth by the means of Scripture, the Holy Spirit, and Christian community, so he teaches us to live out what we speak.

Scripture Is Our Trail Map

Scripture is our reliable map for walking in God's truth. It reveals our ultimate destination. It identifies various paths that will either lead to our destination or get us mired in muck. Scripture shows us the contours of the land, both peaceful pastures and tempting detours, places to rest and pitfalls to avoid. It holds up the promise of divine blessing for those who walk faithfully in God's truth. Remember God's promise to Israel:

> See, I set before you today life and prosperity, death and destruction. For I command you today to love the LORD your God, to walk in his ways, and to keep his commands, decrees and laws; then you will live and increase, and the LORD your God will bless you in the land you are entering to possess. (Deuteronomy 30:15-16, NIV)

As we walk along God's paths, we will avoid death and destruction while enjoying life, prosperity, and blessing. These paths are mapped out for us in the Bible.

I love maps and I love mountains. These two passions interlock when I go hiking. From a map I gain the truth about the region I'm about to explore. That truth guides my steps so that I might fully enjoy a hike in the mountains and return home safely when I'm done.

All serious hikers use U.S. Geological Survey topographical maps—the greenish maps with all of those squiggly elevation lines. (I love "topos" so much that I have the whole state of California on CD-ROM.) The government topographical maps are almost always reliable, though some are a bit dated. It's not uncommon, for example, to find that a hiking trail has changed course since the map was published. Thus, I always take the topos with a grain of salt. A map is reliable only insofar as it is completely up-to-date with the region it depicts.

Although the Bible was written centuries ago, it is still a completely up-to-date map for walking in God's truth. It will show you the best way to walk every time, without fail. Admittedly, sometimes it's hard for us to figure out exactly how to read the biblical map. But God's written Word is always the best map for living and well worth the effort it takes to live according to its truth. In this endeavor we are not alone. God has provided expert assistance through the Holy Spirit.

THE HOLY SPIRIT IS OUR TRAIL GUIDE

As we seek to walk through this life, God gives us not just a trustworthy map but also a trustworthy Guide—his own Spirit. The same Spirit who inspired the writers of Scripture helps us fathom its truth. The same Spirit who guided the great heroes of the Bible also helps us walk in the truth.

If you are hiking into an unfamiliar area, a reliable map is a great friend, but an experienced guide is even better. A dependable escort who knows the trail will always get you there and back without the risks associated with bad map reading or outdated maps. Moreover, a competent guide will point out delights along that trail that you might well have missed if you'd been hiking alone.

Several years ago my family and I were staying in Mammoth Lakes, California, with a young man named Brian, a son of friends in our church. One day I took off to explore a new trail through a lush forest. In places the path became difficult to follow because it snaked through labyrinthine rock formations. My map, as it turned out, was inaccurate in those tricky places, so I took a few wrong turns. With persistence, however, I finally reached the end of the trail.

In the evening I told Brian about my adventure and how much I enjoyed this newly discovered trail. "Have you ever hiked that way?" I asked. "It's really great."

"Well," he responded with embarrassment, "actually I made that trail."

"You did what?" I asked, supposing that I had heard him incorrectly. "You *made* that trail?"

"I did, a couple of years ago. It was my job one summer when I worked for the Forest Service. I explored the forest, chose the best course for the trail, and cleared logs that were in the way. Making the trail was pretty much a solo job."

If only I had known that before I set off with my imprecise map! I wouldn't have lost my way if I had asked Brian to lead me. What better guide could I have had than the person who made the trail in the first place?

So it is in the walk of life. The God who created all things, the God who made you and me, this same God will guide us by his Spirit—if we're willing to pay attention. God provides both the authoritative map and the authoritative Guide for our hike through this world. By relying on both we will walk faithfully in God's truth.

THE COMPANIONSHIP OF CHRISTIAN COMMUNITY

Yet even the most devoted Christians can sometimes get lost. We can misread our map or misconstrue the Spirit's guidance. Though God has provided a perfect guidance system, we are imperfect system operators. We easily project our own desires onto God, and we often confuse our preferences with God's instructions. When left to our own devices, we can walk off the path of divine truth even when we have the best of intentions.

For this reason, God has given us the gift of Christian community. At the moment of conversion, we are baptized into the body of Christ by the Holy Spirit (see 1 Corinthians 12:13). As a member of this body, we find both direction and encouragement for walking in divine truth. When we're not sure where to go, or when we can't read the map correctly, we have others to help us discern God's direction.

Though we should read Scripture privately and though the Holy Spirit dwells within each one of us personally, biblical direction and spiritual guidance are not meant to be individualistic experiences. The Bible is God's gift not only to you, but to the entire church of Jesus Christ. You receive maximum benefit from this gift when you use it in fellowship with other believers. Similarly, the Holy Spirit dwells both in you and in the community of Christians. You will tap the full resources of spiritual guidance only when you are part of a fellowship that faithfully seeks God's direction.[1]

I remember the case of a woman named Clarissa. She was a faithful, mature Christian about thirty years old. As a single woman she had always sought to honor God in her body even though she longed for the sexual fulfillment promised in Scripture for those who are married. When she was tempted to indulge in sexual sin, the combination of Word, Spirit, and Community kept her on the straight and narrow.

But then she started dating a man who was not a believer. Though Clarissa maintained her personal faith, she began to drift away from Christian fellowship and support. Soon she stood alone in her effort to walk in God's truth, and her commitment to sexual purity started to wane. *I've been chaste for so long, and look what that got me—nothing,* Clarissa reasoned. *This time I'm going to do what I want.* So she slept with her boyfriend. Momentary pleasure soon turned to pain when Clarissa discovered that she was pregnant.

She grieved over what she had done. The price of wandering off the divine path was way too high. With an anguished heart, she repented of her sin and committed herself once more to walking in biblical truth.

Clarissa was distressed to learn that her boyfriend had no intention of marrying her and simply assumed that she would get an abortion. But she had always believed abortion to be wrong. Her renewed commitment to scriptural living reinforced this belief. But she was afraid of what her pregnancy might entail—afraid of what people in the church would think, afraid of being a single mother, afraid of giving up her child to adoption, afraid of what would happen if she kept the baby. How tempting it was for Clarissa to abandon her commitment to God's truth once more to secretly have an abortion and return to her normal life.

But this time she didn't try to walk all by herself. She shared her struggle with a few close Christian sisters and with her pastor. She asked for their counsel and prayer as she wrestled with the abortion question. In the end, the trenchant trio of Word, Spirit, and Church combined to help Clarissa walk in God's truth as she perceived it. She decided not to abort her baby but to trust God with her future.

God's path is rarely the easiest one. It wasn't easy for Clarissa to come to church with an increasingly protruding tummy. It wasn't easy for her to admit to people that she was not married and that her baby's father wasn't even part of her life anymore. It wasn't easy to be a single mom to her infant son. But Clarissa was convinced that her earlier failure to walk according to God's truth had been the biggest mistake of her life, and she wasn't going to make that mistake again.

Today, years after Clarissa's ordeal, she is married to a godly man. Her son is thriving. Her life is filled with blessings. But none of this was apparent when she chose to live the truth she believed. She chose the narrow path because she believed it to be God's way—and because she allowed God to direct her steps.

WALKING IN THE TRUTH OF THE GOSPEL

With help from Scripture, Spirit, and Church, we will walk in God's truth. This truth includes all that the Lord has revealed, but it is focused especially in the truth of the gospel. This good news is that God loved us so much that he sent his own Son to be our Savior. The central truth of God is the rock-solid fact of his love for us, his love revealed and extended through Jesus Christ.

Walking in God's truth, therefore, means walking in God's love. Peter made this point in his first letter: "Now that you have purified your souls by your obedience to the truth so that you have genuine mutual love, love one another deeply from the heart" (1:22, NRSV). If we embrace the core of Christian truth—the love of God in Christ—then we must walk in that truth by loving others. It is truth to be obeyed, not just spoken.

How can we love in a way that mirrors the gospel? In countless ways. We love in truth when we teach Sunday school or counsel at junior-high camp or deliver meals to those with a family member in the hospital. We love in truth when we listen to one another's struggles and bear one another's burdens, when we pray for the sick and comfort the brokenhearted. We love in truth when we share the gospel with a colleague at work or build a house with Habitat for Humanity.

Although Clarissa was terrified of the potential reaction of her church to her pregnancy, she was blessed to be in a community that lived out the gospel. People who had experienced God's gracious forgiveness were willing to extend that same grace to Clarissa. Knowing that she had truly repented, they didn't keep reminding her of her sin. Rather, they embraced her, supporting her in her pregnancy and subsequent motherhood. Clarissa's brothers and sisters in Christ walked in the truth of the gospel of God's love.

In his first letter John used a pointed example to elaborate on what it means to love: "[I]f anyone has enough money to live well and sees a brother or sister in need and refuses to help—how can God's love be in that person?" (3:17). He answered his own question by saying, "Dear children, let us not love with words or tongue but with actions and in truth" (3:18, NIV). Although truth-filled love can take a variety of forms, it will be seen when we who are blessed with material possessions share them with others. Generosity is a tangible expression of the truth of the good news of a God who poured out his love so generously in Christ. The more we let the truth of the gospel penetrate our hearts, the more we will be unrestrained in our generous sharing with others. We won't be able to hold back our desire to walk in the truth of God's love.

THE REWARDS OF WALKING IN TRUTH

We should walk in God's truth because it's the right thing to do. Period. But, as is usually the case in things divine, obedience bears delicious fruit.

For example, Psalm 86 connects walking in the truth with *personal whole-ness:* "Teach me your way, O LORD, and I will *walk in your truth;* give me an *undivided heart,* that I may fear your name. I will praise you, O Lord my God, *with all my heart;* I will glorify your name forever" (verses 11-12, NIV). Notice the connection here between walking in truth and having an "undivided heart," a heart wholly de-voted to God.

If you've ever tried to speak God's truth while walking in the opposite direction, you know how painful and ultimately impossible this can be. When we fail to walk in God's truth, our conscience won't leave us alone. It pesters us until we either silence it with hardheartedness or follow its lead back to wholeness. Conversely, when we live according to the truth, we enjoy the peace that accompanies a life of integrity.

When we and those we love walk in God's truth, we also feel *abundant joy.* In the New Testament we read this confession: "I have no greater joy than to hear that my children are walking in the truth" (3 John 4, NIV). Although John was referring to his spiritual children, I can relate to his paternalistic joy when

I think of my own kids. When they choose to do what delights the heart of God, I share in his divine joy. Recently during Vacation Bible School, my children were encouraged to provide financial support for children in Mexico who would like to go to school but can't afford the cost of tuition and supplies. My daughter came home excited about sharing some of her money with these children. Kara opened her bank and found about twenty-seven dollars—a twenty and some ones. Picking up the twenty, she announced, "This is what I'm giving tomorrow." Kara knew very well that by giving away twenty dollars she was sacrificing something she wanted for herself. The next day she and a couple of friends set up a lemonade stand in the front yard so they could raise even more money for the Mexican children. As I watched my daughter walk in the truth of the gospel, my heart echoed the words of John, "I have no greater joy than this."

LIVING TRULY WITHOUT A MASK

When people fail to live the truth they speak, we call them hypocrites. A hypocrite says one thing and does another. Our word *hypocrite* comes from the ancient Greek term *hypokritēs*. Classically, it denoted the actor in a drama who played a role on stage, often wearing a mask as part of a costume. In time *hypokritēs* came to have the negative connotation we associate with the English term *hypocrite*.

In a culture possessed by the demon of image, we can find it terribly tempting to wear masks, to hide our true identity beneath a veneer of words and symbols. Hypocrisy runs rampant on the stage of life. Politicians denounce their foes for financial impropriety only to have their own fiscal chicanery revealed. CEOs promise bright futures for their companies while they secretly sell their stock in anticipation of corporate collapse. Religious leaders decry the sexual immorality of our world until they are caught in the same behavior they have denounced.

Hypocrisy may seem like a harmless drama, but it soon becomes a destructive addiction. Hypocrites end up just like Stanley Ipkiss in the movie *The Mask*. Stanley is a shy, awkward man with a kind heart but a lonely life. When he discovers a magical mask, everything changes. He becomes a swashbuckling daredevil, a lothario who bewitches women with his contrived charm. But after first enjoying his mask-induced transformation, Stanley realizes that his role playing is suicidal. He tries to get rid of the mask, but he just can't do it. He no longer possesses the mask; it possesses him, leading him into increasingly greater peril.[2]

Have you ever felt like Stanley Ipkiss? Have you ever put on a mask only to discover that you can't take it off? Do you ever pretend to be something you're not even though your heart aches for authenticity?

I think of folks in my church who lived for years in bondage to the masks they once chose to wear. One man engaged in repeated affairs while pretending to be an exemplary husband. A woman led everyone to believe that her life was wonderful while she wasted away inside with severe depression. A church leader talked as if he spent time every day in prayer and Bible study when, in reality, he almost never did. All of these people were ensnared by hypocrisy.

Yet they found freedom in Christ. The truth of God's unconditional love penetrated their hearts. Empowered by this love, they confessed their sins and admitted their brokenness. Eventually they risked revealing their true selves to others. By grace they began to live in truth, putting away the masks that had kept them from authentic relationship and genuine healing.

Earlier in this chapter I mentioned how difficult it was for me during my first year of marriage to live out the truth of who I was as a married man. This fact, combined with my father's cancer, made Linda's and my first year of marriage anything but wedded bliss.

I was ashamed of our struggles. In public I wore a "happy Christian husband" mask, but among a few close Christian friends I risked taking off the mask. It felt wonderful to be free from the need to pretend that everything in my life was perfect. Furthermore, my Christian community encouraged Linda and me to get the help we needed to strengthen our relationship.

About two years into our marriage, I was talking with a Christian friend named Matt, who had been married about a year. "So how's it going?" I asked. "How's married life?"

"We're doing great," he said with a smile. "Marriage is such an incredible blessing. It's just amazing."

His answer fit with what I had observed about this perpetually lovey-dovey couple. I felt a bit of envy, I must confess, remembering how Linda and I struggled in our first months. "That's wonderful," I answered. "It's funny, though. Our experience was so different. Our first year was really tough."

Immediately Matt's whole body slumped as if the force of gravity had just doubled. "I'm so glad you said that," he said. "We're having a really crazy time. Marriage is so much harder than I had imagined. I'm feeling discouraged and I don't know what to do."

Suddenly the whole tenor of our conversation changed. Once Matt risked lowering his "happy Christian husband" mask, we were able to speak truthfully. In the end I referred him to a Christian counselor who was able to help Matt and his wife get their marriage on the right track. A couple years later Matt told me he believed that our conversation saved his marriage.

I'm not suggesting that you run out and share your struggles with everyone you meet. But I am urging you to find people with whom you can drop your mask. Yes, it's a risk. But it's a necessary risk.

Moreover, the church of Jesus Christ will be strengthened when we learn to do what the Bible says: share our joys and sorrows with one another, confess our sins to one another, and bear one another's burdens. The masks we wear, the discrepancies between our words and our actions, keep us from experiencing the depth and power of Christian community.

Our commitment to live out the truth we speak will magnify our impact upon the world around us. Perhaps the most common criticism of Christians is that we are hypocrites. Regardless of whether this accusation is fair, the underlying implication is clear: People are looking for authenticity and integrity. They're hungry for people who tell the truth and live it. They'll be inclined to listen to us if our mouths and our feet deliver the same message, if we speak *and* live consistently according to God's truth.

It is to the world-changing potential of truthfulness that we turn in the next chapter.

LIVING AS CHILDREN
OF LIGHT

THE MAGNETISM OF TRUTH IN A DARK WORLD

It's funny how much kids love flashlights. When my family and I go camping, my kids prize their inexpensive flashlights as if they were priceless treasures. They shine them with glee. They fret over misplacing them. They clutch them when falling asleep. There's just about nothing better for a child than having a flashlight when day turns to night.

Though I left chronological childhood behind decades ago, I still adore flashlights. If you searched through my belongings, you'd find at least a dozen of them. (In fact, I just bought a high-intensity halogen beauty last week.) My very first flashlight was a gleaming chrome model with a switch that doubled as a magnet. I could do amazing things with that flashlight. By holding it steady in a tent and thumping my sleeping bag, I could watch millions of dust particles dance in the air. By pointing the light at a friend and shaking it rhythmically, I could imitate a silent movie. By closing my mouth around the end of the flashlight, I could make a monster face to scare my sister. By shining my light into the forest, I could vanquish the powers of darkness. And with the magnetic switch, I could make paper clips dance as if by magic or stick my flashlight to the steel frame of my camp bunk so it wouldn't get lost.

It's great to be a child with a flashlight. According to Scripture, however, we possess something even better. By God's grace, *we've become children of the light.* "For once you were darkness," Paul wrote, "but now in the Lord you are light.

Live as children of light" (Ephesians 5:8, NRSV). When we put our faith in Jesus Christ, we get something better than a flashlight. We receive a completely new identity as people of light.

That's stunning news. But what difference will it make in our daily lives? According to Jesus, we should shine our light into the darkness much as children wield their flashlights in a pitch-black forest. How can we do this? How can we live as children of light in a dark world?

Let's explore four dimensions of living as children of light. The more we experience these dimensions, the more we will be the people God has called us to be. But our own personal fulfillment is only the beginning. By living as light in the world, we have a marvelous—indeed, unprecedented—opportunity to make a difference. Through you, the light of God will illumine that which is now shrouded in shadow and needs to be seen clearly. And, as you shine with the light of truth, people will be drawn not only to you but also to the God who is the source of your distinctive brightness. So, for the sake of our souls and for the sake of the world, let's explore the four dimensions of being children of light.

AVOIDING THE SINISTER PATH

The first dimension concerns what we do *not* do. After calling us to live as children of light, Paul added, "[F]or the fruit of the light is found in all that is good and right and true. Try to find out what is pleasing to the Lord. Take no part in the unfruitful works of darkness." (Ephesians 5:9-11, NRSV). John concurred in his first letter: "God is light and in him there is no darkness at all. If we say that we have fellowship with him while we are walking in darkness, we lie and do not do what is true" (1:5-6, NRSV). As children of light we must intentionally and continually refuse to walk in darkness. It's just not possible to stroll in light and darkness simultaneously.

Therefore, as children of light we stop walking in darkness only by turning from a lifestyle of sin in general and from sinful deception in particular. As we saw in the previous chapter, the Bible employs the metaphor of walking to signify our lifestyle. Walking in darkness is not occasional sin, but a pattern of sin. We are not walking in darkness, for example, if we tell a lie once in a while. But if we do it repeatedly, so that falsehood becomes an integral part of our lives, then we have chosen the sinister path.

Both Paul and John linked light to truth. "The fruit of the *light*," Paul explained, "is found in all that is good and right and *true*" (Ephesians 5:9, NRSV). According to John, if we claim to have fellowship with God while walking in darkness, we "do not do *what is true*" (1 John 1:6, NRSV). Scripture makes this same connection elsewhere. The psalmist prayed, "O send out your light and your truth; let them lead me" (Psalm 43:3, NRSV). The gospel of John explains that "those who do what is true come to the light" (3:21; NRSV). Truth and light, light and truth—the two are inseparable. Both ultimately radiate from God's own being as the brilliantly Truthful Trinity.

Therefore, as children of light who reject worldly darkness, we must turn from a lifestyle of sin in general and from deception in particular. This fits with what we saw in chapter 3 about spurning spin as a prerequisite to embracing the truth. We can't hope to be people of light and truth if we willingly lurk in the shadows of falsehood.

LET YOUR LIGHT SHINE IN THE DARKNESS

Throughout history, religious folk have sought to reject secular darkness by separating themselves from this world. Consider, for instance, a group of Jews who lived during the time of Jesus. To keep from being tainted by the world, they isolated themselves in the barren wilderness near the Dead Sea. These religious separatists saw the world as a battle between the "Prince of Lights" and the "Angel of Darkness." Those who sought to walk on the "paths of light" could join their "Community of truth," becoming one of the "sons of light" or "sons of truth."[1] How were they to live as people of light and truth in a dark world? Their first rule was, "They should *keep apart from men of sin* in order to constitute a Community in law and possessions."[2] The one who joined this community "should swear by the covenant *to be segregated from all the men of sin* who walk along paths of irreverence."[3] Though they lived in the physical world, these sons of light were to withdraw from the world of people as much as possible, thus protecting the light and truth from the onslaught of darkness.

Jesus disagreed with this isolationist option. He called his followers to live in the dark world so that they might illumine it.

> You are the light of the world. A city built on a hill cannot be hid. No one after lighting a lamp puts it under the bushel basket, but on the lampstand, and it gives light to all in the house. In the same way, let your light shine before others, so that they may see your good works and give glory to your Father in heaven. (Matthew 5:14-16, NRSV)

Whereas the Jewish separatists said, "Keep apart from men of sin," Jesus said, "Let your light shine before others," that is, in the presence of the sinful people of this dark world. Jesus taught that we are the light, and not the light of some cloistered community, but the light of the world. Thus, we must reject both the darkness of the world and the temptation to separate ourselves completely from it.

Although relatively few Christians today abandon human society completely, many of us unintentionally segregate ourselves from people who live in darkness. All of our friends are Christians. All of our activities revolve around the church. Even though we brush up against nonbelievers at work or in our neighborhoods, we rarely spend much time with them. As a pastor I easily fall into this trap and must continually monitor my faithfulness to the call of Jesus to shine into the world. I am grateful for the relationships I develop outside of church: helping in my children's school, rooting for their soccer teams, or just hanging out in my favorite coffee shop.

Once we're positioned in the world of darkness, how can we allow our light to shine? Jesus said, "Let your light shine before others, so that they may see your good works and give glory to your Father in heaven" (Matthew 5:16, NRSV). We are to do good works in the world in such a way that its people give glory to God.

As a Protestant Christian I get a little queasy when talking about good works. I'm all too aware of the historic tendency—indeed, my own tendency—to minimize grace and maximize human efforts to earn God's favor. Fearful of turning the Christian life into a legalistic enterprise, some Christians avoid talking about good works altogether. But since Jesus says we're to do good works, we can't just ignore them. Yet notice carefully their context and purpose: We do good deeds not in order to become the light of the world, but because we *already are* that light. By grace we have been delivered from darkness to light, and by grace we should live as children of light. Our purpose is not to earn God's favor, but to live out that favor so that others may glorify God.

Some Christians use Jesus' emphasis on good works as an excuse not to talk about God. "I don't feel comfortable talking about my faith," they explain, "so I simply do works of charity and justice for God's glory." At first this sounds noble, but it misses Jesus' point. If we do good works without mentioning God, what will encourage observers of our efforts to give God the glory? Won't they be more inclined to give *us* the praise that God deserves? Our light will radiate effectively in this world only when our good works complement our verbal witness. Good deeds without truth, truth without good deeds—each of these incomplete combinations shines only dimly.

How grateful I am for Christian ministries that meet the tangible needs of people while unapologetically proclaiming the truth of the gospel. I think, for example, of one of my church's ministry partners, Tijuana Christian Mission. Under the leadership of Martha Lopez, this ministry provides food, shelter, and education for disadvantaged children while at the same time telling them about Jesus. Tijuana Christian Mission is not unique in this regard. Countless churches, parachurch organizations, and individual Christians amplify their good deeds with biblical truth in such a way that the light of Christ penetrates the darkness.

What about you? Are you living in the world so that those around you might see God's light reflected in you? Or have you sequestered yourself within the cloistered safety of Christian community? Are you letting your light shine by doing good works interpreted by evangelical truth? If, as you honestly examine your life, the answer is no, then I urge you to let your light shine fully. Ask the Lord to help you live in this world for his glory. Begin now to pray for at least one significant relationship with an unbeliever. Ask the Holy Spirit to guide you into a place of ministry that links good deeds with Christian truth. Remember, as a child of the light you must let your light shine into the darkness.

EXPOSING THE UNFRUITFUL WORKS OF DARKNESS

We have seen already that the first dimension of living as children of light involves not walking in darkness. Yet we must not conclude that we should have no interaction with darkness at all. According to Paul, we are to "[t]ake no part in the unfruitful works of darkness, but instead *expose them*" (Ephesians 5:11, NRSV). The Greek verb translated "to expose" means "to reveal" or "to prosecute" as in a law court. Thus, we don't stand back at a safe distance from evil. Instead, we shine the light of truth upon it, revealing its diabolical nature. As Paul explained, "[E]verything exposed by the light becomes visible" (Ephesians 5:13, NRSV). When illumined by God's truth, evil can't continue to hide in the shadows.

We find a telling example of truth exposing evil in J. R. R. Tolkien's *The Lord of the Rings,* a masterful story depicting the struggle between light and darkness. On the side of light are Gandalf the wizard, King Théoden, and their partners. Opposed to them are Sauron—the Dark Lord—and a host of evil creatures, including a turncoat wizard named Saruman. In his lust for power, Saruman wages war against the forces of righteousness, slaughtering many good people until, at last, they vanquish him.

When Gandalf, Théoden, and their allies confront the defeated Saruman in his fortress, they are stunned to hear not the abrasive rant of a tyrant, but the soothing voice of a sage. Saruman's words, sweet as honey, bewitch his righteous opponents. Soon Gandalf's followers find themselves strangely drawn to the evil wizard, and they begin to despise their own faithful leader. Their perception of right and wrong has been inverted by Saruman's unexpected charm.

While Saruman speaks, King Théoden is strangely silent, seemingly drunk on the liquor of his enemy's words. When the evil wizard invites Théoden into a partnership of "peace and friendship," it appears the king will accept the offer.

"We will have peace," Théoden whispers in apparent acquiescence. Then, as if finally regaining his senses, he continues strongly, "We will have peace, when you and all your works have perished.... You are a liar, Saruman, and a corrupter of men's hearts."[4]

At first, the king's own soldiers are dismayed. Their master's voice seems harsh when compared to that of Saruman. Finally, Gandalf intervenes, shining the light of truth upon Saruman's deception—and Saruman's evil nature is exposed. Only then do the soldiers regain an accurate perception of truth and falsehood.

What breaks the power of Saruman's spell and protects good people from the snare of evil's deception? Only Gandalf's courage to shine the truth into the darkness, revealing evil for what it is.

You and I are called to be like Gandalf. We live in a world replete with the unfruitful works of darkness, including alluring, deceptive speech. These works must be exposed by divine truth. Yet, as we speak the truth, we will often sound harsh and uncharitable.

For example, our world overflows with the sweet sentiments of greeting-card religiosity:

God is love, and God's love fills everybody.

It doesn't matter what you believe as long as you believe sincerely.

People find God at the end of many different paths, and that's beautiful.

Let's stop talking about evil, sin, and all that judgmental stuff. People are basically good, and if we just understand one another, then we'll all live in peace.

Such saccharine statements are commonplace. They are also false in light of the following biblical truths.

God's love extends to all people, but it only fills those who through faith
in Christ have been transformed by the Holy Spirit.

It matters profoundly what a person believes since salvation comes
through Jesus Christ alone.

Though people may have a spiritual experience through different religions, Jesus is "the way, the truth, and the life" (John 14:6). *Only*
through him do we come to true knowledge of God.

We mustn't stop talking about evil and sin, because these define our fundamental human problem. True peace—with God and among people—
will come not through mutual understanding, but through Jesus Christ,
the One who has forged reconciliation through his death on the cross.

Admittedly, these statements can sound harsh compared to the syrupy sentiments they refute. Those who hear us take a stand for God's truth will often
condemn what they take to be our narrow-mindedness and intolerance. Yet if
we fail to shine the light of God's truth upon the clichés of politically correct
religion, then we'll allow falsehood to reign while keeping our neighbors from
genuine relationship with God. In a culture that denies the existence of absolute truth, we need to speak the truth that there is one God, that our fundamental human problem is far deeper than a lack of understanding, and that
God has dealt with the problem of sin through Jesus Christ, "the Savior of
the world" (1 John 4:14).

By shining the light of divine revelation into our world, we will expose evil
in many forms. Racism will be revealed as sinful hatred. Materialism will be
uncovered as greed. Pornography will be seen not as artistic freedom, but as a
pernicious denial of human dignity. Workaholism will be exposed as a failure to
trust God and to live according to his priorities. Of course, if we are to expose
the unfruitful works of darkness, we must first shine the light of truth upon our
own lives, renouncing our own sin and the ways we rationalize it. Hypocrisy

will dim our light in an instant. As children of the light, we must expose the unfruitful works of darkness, both through our words and through light-filled living.

INVITING OTHERS INTO THE LIGHT OF CHRIST

Some Christians get so carried away with exposing the works of darkness that they forget the ultimate purpose of this activity. The goal is not condemnation, but redemption. After urging us to "take no part in the unfruitful works of darkness, but instead expose them" (Ephesians 5:11, NRSV), Paul concludes with this surprising invitation:

> Sleeper, awake!
>> Rise from the dead,
> and Christ will shine on you. (verse 14, NRSV)

Although he was writing to Christians, Paul quoted a poem that was originally addressed to unbelievers who were, therefore, sleeping in darkness. But these people are not beyond hope. They can wake up to new life in the light of Christ. We who have already awakened must pass on the message of hope to those who desperately need it. Thus, the fourth dimension of living as children of light is inviting the children of darkness to join us in the light.

Once again, this Christian commitment to call others into the light contrasts starkly with the convictions of the Jewish separatists at the Dead Sea. They believed that God himself had "put an everlasting loathing" between themselves and the "sons of darkness." Those within the community of truth should "love all the sons of light" and "detest the sons of darkness." They anticipated a war between good and evil that would result in the ultimate destruction of the sons of darkness at the hands of the sons of light. They even spoke of this attack upon the people of darkness as "shining" or "illuminating" the earth.[5]

Jesus says that we are to let our light shine not to annihilate those trapped in darkness, but so that those in darkness might recognize and glorify God.

Paul exemplified this evangelical impulse by inviting the sleeper to arise and live in the light of Christ. As children of light, we shine in the world so that those who live in darkness might see and come to the light. Even when we expose the works of darkness, our ultimate purpose is to redeem people blinded by the darkness and guide them into the brilliance of God's light.

No matter how blind they may seem, we must never give up on those who are lost in darkness. Rather, we must persevere in our effort to lead them to the light. When we're inclined to give up on people, we should remember that God can redeem even the one who seems beyond hope. If you had known Zacchaeus, the dishonest, greedy, traitorous tax collector, would you have expected him to follow Jesus? And what about Saul, the zealous persecutor of the early church? Would you have shone the light of Christ in Saul's direction in the expectation of his becoming a passionate evangelist for Christ? Or consider C. S. Lewis, the arrogant, academic atheist. If you had stood in the shoes of Lewis's close friend J. R. R. Tolkien, would you have shared Christian truth with Lewis in the hope of his conversion? Or would you have figured that Lewis was a lost cause?

Two years ago I met an up-and-coming scientist named Carolyn. She made an appointment with me because, as she said, "I have lots and lots of questions about Christianity." Indeed, she did—a seemingly endless list. Carolyn's queries were far deeper than the usual ones. She had obviously done her homework, having studied the Bible, Christian theology, and several world religions. Her interrogation of me was fair, but tough and thorough. As I got to know a bit more about Carolyn, I must confess that I felt despair over her coming to faith in Christ. For one thing, she was a gifted doctoral student in chemistry who thrived in a materialistic, cerebral environment. For another, she was Jewish. If she were to confess Jesus as the Messiah, she would alienate herself from her family and many of her friends. In my experience, intellectual Jewish doctoral students don't become Christians. Nevertheless, in my first meeting with Carolyn and in subsequent conversations with her, I tried to shine the light of truth upon her questions. I prayed regularly for her, asking the Lord to draw her to himself in spite of many contrary pressures. I made every effort to be faithful as a child of the light, leaving the results to God.

About a year after my first meeting with Carolyn, *I* was asking her *my* list of questions: "Do you believe in Jesus Christ as your Lord and Savior?" "Will you live as his disciple?" "Will you be a faithful member of his church?" "By what name will you be baptized today?" Jesus had drawn Carolyn into his radiance, and she had become a child of the light. I had the privilege of baptizing her and welcoming her as a member of our church.

THE ATTRACTION OF THE LIGHT

What made the difference for Carolyn? My answers to her questions contributed in some small way to her conversion. Her own effort in seeking the truth added considerably to the mix. But, according to Carolyn's own testimony, the primary influence upon her journey to Christian faith was the light shone by Christians in her life. In college Carolyn became friends with several believers in Jesus. Their kindness and integrity impressed her. Their honesty about all things, including their faith, drew Carolyn closer to the Lord.

Throughout this book I have suggested that our truthfulness will attract people to Christ. And I don't mean only telling the truth about the gospel. Truthfulness in general, especially about the things we'd rather hide, draws unbelievers to God like a magnet. That's a major reason why the *walk* of truth—living the truth as well as speaking it—is so essential. Conversely, our failure to speak and live the truth repels people from the light.

Consider the tragic situation in the Roman Catholic Church today. The fact that scores of priests have molested children is a scandal in its own right. But the disgrace has been multiplied by the failure of church officials to speak truthfully about this calamity. Trust in the church has plunged because the church hierarchy chose silence over truth. As a result, people have been repelled from the light rather than drawn to it.

Of course, the scourge of concealed abuse has tainted Protestant churches as well. I am aware of leaders in my own denomination who exacerbated the offense of a pastor's sexual sin by concealing what he had done. But I have also seen church leaders choose the way of truthfulness in similar situations. Several years ago a major Protestant church in Southern California discovered that one of its leading elders, a veritable pillar of the church, had been molesting young girls in the congregation. When he confessed his offenses to church officials, they took decisive action. First, they exercised church discipline with the offending leader. Second, anticipating how this matter would make headlines, they called a press conference to set matters straight. They told the truth about what had happened and how they had responded to the situation. They avoided rationalizations and excuses, even though what their former leader had done reflected poorly upon the church.

I watched carefully to see how the secular news media would react to these events. I expected reporters to go after this story like wolves feasting on an injured deer. Indeed, the story appeared in the papers and on local news channels. But the tone of every report I witnessed was surprisingly subdued. Church officials were praised for their openness. What appeared to threaten the reputation of a fine church turned out to strengthen it. Truthfulness, even in such an embarrassing situation, commended this church and its Lord in the eyes of the world.

I was inspired by the example of this church several years later when confronting a painfully trying problem in my own congregation. It was a personnel matter that involved not moral failure by a staff member, but an utter mismatch between her gifts and the congregation's needs. Herculean efforts by our personnel experts couldn't solve the problem. So, after months of intense conversation, we were finally able to work out an agreement whereby the staff member would resign and we would be generous in caring for her financial needs. Yet the rules of our church demanded that the final agreement be approved by the whole congregation, not just church leaders.

As you can well imagine, we who were in charge of the congregational meeting struggled to know what to say. Many personnel matters are, by kindness and by law, confidential. We really couldn't explain in detail where the staff member had failed in her job performance. Yet we felt compelled to be as truthful as possible, especially about our own mistakes.

That congregational meeting was one of the hardest experiences of my ministry. I can't remember a time when I felt more conscious of relying upon the Holy Spirit for guidance in speaking the truth. Not only did I admit several of my own shortcomings as a leader, but I was publicly reprimanded by those in the congregation who were, for the most part, unaware of the facts of the case. They were sure, however, that the root problem was my failure as a supervisor. I tried to be as honest as possible and to accept criticism where it was valid.

During the meeting I noticed a couple I didn't recognize. Were they news reporters? Were they attorneys ready to pounce on us? Worse yet, were they first-time visitors to our church who accidentally found themselves mired in our personnel swamp?

When the meeting finally ended, this couple walked up to me.

"Hello," they began, "we're Pete and Val. We're visiting your church today for the first time."

"Oh no," I said. "I'm so sorry you stumbled into this mess. I can't imagine how we could have made a poorer impression. Please don't judge us by this meeting."

"On the contrary," they responded. "We stayed for the meeting because we wanted to see how your church handled tough issues. We were impressed with how fair and open you and the other leaders were. You risked a lot to tell the truth and yet to be kind to the person who is leaving. It shows how much you value your congregation and trust them. We've pretty much decided to join your church because of what we've seen here today."

I was stunned. With tears in my eyes, I thanked Pete and Val for their encouragement. Silently I thanked the Lord for this special bit of grace. In my hour of deep discouragement, he had affirmed the choice to be truthful even when it required all the strength I could muster—and far more. Without the Spirit's help, I doubt I would have been able to make it through that congregational meeting without blowing up in a burst of defensiveness.

In our time of history, in our world that is drowning in spin, people are hungry for truth. Sickened by the intentional deception of spin, they're yearning for authenticity. They need something or someone to trust. This puts us in an optimal position as children of light. God calls us to be truthful—and therefore trustworthy—people. With the help of the Holy Spirit, we can speak and live the truth, even when it requires superhuman strength. If we live truthfully as individual Christians, and if our churches abound with authenticity, then outsiders will be drawn to us. More important, they will be attracted to our Savior who is the Truth and the Light. If we have been truthful in our words and our deeds, then we will have earned the trust of our neighbors. They will be inclined to believe us when we speak of God's grace in Christ because we are people who tell and live the truth.

Of course, I'm not suggesting that every unbeliever will immediately be impressed by truthfulness. Many are so ensnared in the web of spin that they'll be unable to free themselves. But countless people, even those who are unreservedly secular, will want to associate themselves with people who embody truthfulness. After all, every person was created by a truthful God to be a person of truth. In spite of the fallenness of our world and the corruption of the human heart, we long to be who we were meant to be and to live in fellowship with the Truthful Trinity.

You might be tempted to accuse me of wishful spiritual thinking at this point, but I have the eminently secular *Time* magazine backing me up. *Time* recently recognized three women as "Persons of the Year," three "Whistleblowers," as *Time* calls them.[6] I would prefer to call them *truth speakers*. Cynthia Cooper of WorldCom, Coleen Rowley of the FBI, and Sherron Watkins of Enron were recognized for telling the truth when no one wanted to hear it. At the risk of their jobs, these women dared to be true. And in doing so, they offended many colleagues. I've said all along that truthfulness is costly. But the countercultural honesty of Cooper, Rowley, and Watkins so impressed *Time* that it awarded them the coveted title of "Persons of the Year." Even people who don't act like these three women are nevertheless fascinated by them and drawn magnetically by their commitment to honesty.

People are attracted to the light of truth like moths to a lantern. During a recent camping trip, I was fascinated to watch moths flock around my Coleman lantern only seconds after I lighted it. For hours they'd flit about the glass, trying in vain to reach the brilliant, glowing mantles. Of course, this lantern analogy breaks down because if the moths actually touched the light they sought, they'd instantly die. When people touch the Light of the World through faith, however, they instantly live. "I am the light of the world," Jesus said. "Whoever follows me will never walk in darkness but will have the light of life" (John 8:12, NRSV). By reflecting the light of Christ into the dark world through our truthfulness, we will attract people to the One who is the Light, the Way, the Truth, and the Life.

You are a child of the light. Though you live in a world of darkness, you don't need to walk in it any longer. Yet you mustn't hide your light by removing yourself from the people who still live in darkness. God has sent you into the dark world where light is so desperately needed. So let your light shine. Expose empty words and dark deeds with divine truth.

If you are truthful in all things, many will flock to the light that shines through you. Yes, you will be a bearer of bad news at times, the news that, without Christ, we are all asleep, even dead. But you are also privileged to deliver the good news. The true Light of the World has become flesh in Jesus, the One who brings grace and truth into a dark world. Thus, with the apostle Paul we invite the one living in darkness into the light:

Sleeper, awake!
    Rise from the dead,
and Christ will shine on you. (Ephesians 5:14, NRSV)

ENJOY THE FREEDOM
OF TRUTH

How Truthful Living Sets You Free

When I arrived at the retreat center, my sense of anticipation took a beating as I noticed that several groups were sharing the facility that weekend. I had planned a meditative weekend retreat for a group from my church and didn't want to be disturbed by others. But I found that, as we began our activities on Friday evening, it seemed as if we had the whole place to ourselves. The conference grounds were expansive enough to accommodate several groups at once without making us step all over one another.

I arose early on Saturday morning to get some quiet time at breakfast. Soon, however, I was approached by a woman I didn't recognize, someone from one of the other groups, I surmised.

"May I join you?" she asked.

Not wanting to be rude, I said, "Sure."

She sat down and introduced herself. "Hi, my name is Sandy. I'm a neurotic."

Just about choking on my cereal, I managed somehow to respond politely. "Hi, Sandy. I'm Mark. Nice to meet you." *This is just great,* I thought. *I wanted some time alone, and now I'm stuck with a chatty mental case.*

After eating in silence for several minutes, we were joined by a man I didn't know. Pulling up a chair, he introduced himself. "Hi, my name's Rick, and I'm an overeater."

As Sandy happily introduced herself as a neurotic, I felt utterly out of place. I knew that I'd better not crack a joke about how many pieces of bacon Rick was having for breakfast. But merely saying, "Hi, Rick. I'm Mark" seemed woefully inadequate. I felt as if I should have blurted out, "Hi, my name's Mark, and I've got a lot of problems too."

As I listened to Sandy and Rick talk over breakfast, I realized they were part of a collection of people at the retreat center from various twelve-step groups patterned after Alcoholics Anonymous. Sandy was part of Neurotics Anonymous, and Rick was a member of Overeaters Anonymous. They had assumed that I was also part of their larger group.

Once I got over my awkwardness, I explained to my breakfast companions that I was leading a spiritual retreat for people from my church. They didn't seem to mind that I wasn't a part of their retreat and continued to talk openly about their personal struggles and victories. I marveled at their openness. They avoided the superficiality that plagues new relationships, honestly sharing the kind of things most of us work hard to hide. They were free in a way I was not, that's for sure. I found myself envying their courageous, calm truthfulness about what mattered most in their lives.

YEARNING FOR FREEDOM

Sandy and Rick had broken free from the cultural imperative to look good on the outside, no matter what. We live in a society that worships the idol of image. Public relations experts make big bucks helping politicians, programs, and products look much better than they actually are. I once met a man whose job it was to take the pictures of food you see in advertisements. He explained how, when doing a photo shoot for a major fast-food chain, he had sorted through hundreds of hamburger buns looking for the perfect model for his picture. After hours of sorting, he found the ideal bun, not to mention the pristine lettuce leaf and tomato slice. Then he cooked dozens of patties to create the perfect one. After assembling the ideal burger, he covered it with preservatives and glossy chemicals that made it unfit for human consumption and, I might add, utterly unlike anything customers would actually see this side of fast-food paradise. That perfect—and perfectly unrealistic—image sold millions of burgers to people like you and me.

Before we accuse PR experts of image idolatry, however, we must examine our own behavior. We often try hard to make a good impression by looking better than we really are or acting nicer than we usually act. We purchase cars that exceed our needs and budgets because they look impressive. We chat about our successes and conveniently downplay our failures. We act like ideal Christians at church, while we hide our pains and struggles. We make sure our clothing displays the right logos. We suck in our guts. We camouflage our faces with makeup. We color our graying hair and minimize our receding hairlines. We strive to cover up our aging bodies, not to mention our faults, fears, family secrets, and failures. We create a meticulously manicured image for ourselves, and we labor diligently to project and protect it. Often we're no more authentic than a picture of the perfect hamburger.

Yet, deep inside, we yearn for the freedom to be who we are, to be seen, warts and all, to share ourselves genuinely with others so that we might experience what it feels like to be understood and accepted. We ache for the freedom to be truthful about ourselves. This is what I felt that morning at the retreat center. In spite of my penchant for privacy, deep within I longed to be able to share my struggles with two complete strangers, so that Sandy and Rick could offer me the same support and encouragement they graciously gave each other.

Furthermore, there is a second level of freedom that is deeper than authenticity—a profound freedom that releases us from our struggles, sins, and scars. Don't you long to be released from the bondage of your past, from the sins that plague you, from the obsession to seek human approval, from the addictions that rule your life, from the fears that keep you from living fully? Don't you yearn to be free, truly free?

Ultimate Freedom

Jesus said, "So if the Son sets you free, you will indeed be free" (John 8:36). He promises not just the image of freedom, but genuine freedom. What an astounding promise! Jesus offers to fulfill the deepest longing of our hearts. But how do we accept his offer so that we can experience true freedom?

His stirring promise appears in the eighth chapter of John's gospel, a chapter that helps us understand the nature of and the path to freedom. This chapter begins with the moving account of a woman caught in adultery. Discovered in the midst of a shameful offense, indeed, a capital offense according to Jewish law, this woman was condemned by the Pharisees, who sought to stone her. But Jesus intervened, confronting her accusers with their own guilt and setting the woman free. "Go and sin no more," Jesus told the woman he had just pardoned from execution (John 8:11).

What sort of freedom does Jesus offer? Freedom from judgment, from shame, from death, from the drive to keep on sinning.

After releasing the adulterous woman, Jesus turned to the crowd. "I am the light of the world," he told them. "If you follow me, you won't be stumbling through the darkness, because you will have the light that leads to life" (John 8:12). Jesus, the Light of the World, offers freedom from stumbling through life, freedom from the domination of darkness, freedom from lifeless living.

As John 8 continues, Jesus presented himself not only as the Light of the World but also as the Son of Man who would be lifted up on the cross. Many in the crowd came to believe in Jesus at this point. To these new believers Jesus said, "If you continue in my word, you are truly my disciples; and you will know the truth, and the truth will make you free" (verses 31-32, NRSV). Here is the path to true freedom. First, believe in Jesus. Second, continue in his Word. Let's scrutinize the steps of this path more closely.

The Freedom of Complete Trust

If we are to be free, we must first believe in Jesus. Believing in him begins with affirming the right things about him, but it goes much further. Believing in Jesus means not only that we acknowledge his multifaceted identity as Lord and Savior but also that we personally entrust ourselves to him as *our* Lord and Savior. Based upon what we believe about Jesus, faith is putting our full trust in him.

Consider, for example, the roles Jesus mentioned in John 8: Son of Man and Light of the World. Jesus was lifted up on the cross as the Son of Man in order to take the judgment for humanity's sin upon himself. As the Son of Man, he offered himself unto death, and, therefore, he offers us freedom from sin. Believing in him means we relinquish all attempts to save ourselves and rely upon him alone for salvation. Once we do this, we experience freedom from sin and its lethal results.

Jesus also presents himself as the Light of the World. Believing in him means we accept his light for our own lives, following his guidance and walking along the path he illumines. When Jesus is the light of our lives, we enjoy freedom from stumbling along in the darkness of this world. Through faith in him we begin to experience "life in all its fullness" (John 10:10).[1]

The Freedom of Continual Following

Believing in Jesus, however essential it may be, is not the goal, but the starting point of new life. After entering this new life by faith, we *live it* by continuing in Jesus' Word. The Greek verb rendered "to continue" means "to remain" in a place for an extended period of time. If my children spoke New Testament Greek, rather than asking to sleep over at a friend's house, they'd ask to "continue" there. This Greek verb appears later in the gospel of John to highlight the primacy and benefits of our relationship with Jesus:

> *Remain* in me, and I will *remain* in you.... Those who *remain* in me,
> and I in them, will produce much fruit.... [I]f you *stay joined* to me
> and my words *remain* in you, you may ask any request you like, and it
> will be granted!... I have loved you even as the Father has loved me.
> *Remain* in my love. When you obey me, you *remain* in my love. (John
> 15:4,5,7,9-10).

When Jesus speaks of us continuing in his Word, therefore, he refers not to a temporary choice or a fleeting feeling, but to a lifetime of deep, abiding connectedness to his Word.

What is this Word? Most precisely, it is Jesus' own teaching. This teaching encapsulates the more extensive Word of Jesus, which is the truth found throughout the Scripture, the written Word of God. We continue in the Word of Jesus when we read, study, meditate upon, and live out both what Jesus himself taught and the teaching found throughout the Bible.

Jesus said, "If you continue in my word, *you are truly my disciples*" (John 8:31, NRSV). Disciples are students of a master, apprentices who learn to imitate the master's craft through a committed relationship with him. Disciples of Jesus spend time with him, learning both his craft and his character, becoming like him so that they might act like him. As disciples we continue in the Word of Jesus to absorb his way of thinking, to imitate his way of being, and to know him more intimately. As this happens, obedience to his directives becomes instinctual because the Holy Spirit has conformed our minds and hearts to Christ.

Are you continuing in the multifaceted Word of Jesus? Are you regularly immersing yourself in Scripture, including but not limited to the actual teachings of Jesus? If not, then you are missing out on the freedom he offers. Why not begin today to examine, reflect upon, absorb, and carry out biblical truth?

If you study the Bible faithfully, are you doing so in order to have your heart transformed or merely to amass a larger body of theological truth? Are you allowing Scripture to lead you into a deeper relationship with Jesus, the living Word of God? Or has Bible study become like brushing your teeth, something you do because you know you should, but not because you expect it to change your life? I must confess that I easily fall into this trap. I catch myself rushing to get through my appointed Bible passages as if checking them off my to-do list were the main point. Yet, since I seek to be a true disciple of my Master and since I long for the freedom he offers, I must learn to slow down and, as my friend Ben Patterson suggests, *marinate* myself in the tangy Word of God.

EMANCIPATED BY THE TRUTH

According to Jesus, if you remain in his Word, you will "know the truth, and the truth will set you free" (John 8:32). The truth that leads to freedom is the truth of God's revelation, the truth of Scripture. More pointedly, it's the truth of the gospel, the good news that leads to freedom from sin, judgment, and eternal death. Yet divine truth is never merely propositional. It's always personal. The truth that sets us free is, ultimately, the One who is "the way, the truth, and the life" (John 14:6).

It seems counterintuitive to accept Jesus' assertion that freedom comes from the truth. It's certainly countercultural. Our world insists that real freedom results from escaping the narrow constraints of truth. According to our cultural mythology, we are liberated only when we freely choose which truth to embrace—typically a version of "truth" that enhances our personal comfort. Freedom means acting autonomously, untrammeled by conventional morality. Freedom is spontaneous self-determination. It doesn't come from conforming to some authoritative revealed truth outside of ourselves, as Jesus claimed.

French intellectual Catherine Millet has become the poster child for this view of freedom. Her autobiography focuses upon her manifold sexual exploits, experienced apart from the constraints of custom, commitment, and morality. What motivated such gross sexual adventurism? "I was carried by the conviction that I rejoiced in extraordinary freedom," she explains.[2] But Millet isn't satisfied to enjoy her own freedom quietly. She published her autobiography to encourage others to pursue the same type of freedom: "I have a fantasy that sexual relations could be possible with the entire scope of the human family, that it can be just as easy and generous as offering one's seat to an elderly woman on the subway."[3]

Millet exemplifies the pursuit of freedom *apart from* truth, not the freedom that *comes from* truth. The freedom of Jesus, on the contrary, is not license to throw off all constraint, to pursue a self-directed life, to flaunt decency and morality. Rather, the freedom of Jesus is tethered to the foundational, bottom-line truth—the truth of the gospel, the truth of who God really is, the truth of who God created us to be.

When it comes to our sexuality, for example, authentic freedom is not the ability to do with our bodies whatever strikes our fancy. Rather, sexual freedom follows from the truth of who we are as beings created in God's image for God's own glory. Our bodies are not toys for pleasure, but temples for praise. God will be glorified in our sexuality, and we will experience the fullest joy when we act according to his intention. The Bible shows us that sexual intimacy is to be experienced only within the context of a committed, loving marriage. Though it is always right to offer one's seat to an elderly woman on the subway, it is never right to have sex with any woman unless she is your wife.

Our culture says, "Freedom comes when we're unhindered by the constraints of truth." Jesus says, "You will know the truth, and the truth will set you free" (John 8:32). Commenting on these words, Pope John Paul II wrote in his first encyclical,

> These words contain both a fundamental requirement and a warning: the requirement of an honest relationship with regard to truth as a condition for authentic freedom, and the warning to avoid every kind of illusory freedom, every superficial unilateral freedom, every freedom that fails to enter into the whole truth about man and the world.[4]

John Paul II is right. The apparent freedom of this world, epitomized by Catherine Millet, is illusory, superficial, and truthless. I can't begin to tell you how many people have come to me throughout my years as a pastor to seek healing for sexual brokenness. At one time they had bought into the world's promise of sexual freedom, but after heartbreak, betrayal, disease, desertion, unwanted pregnancies, and abortion, they found it to be not only empty, but life destroying. Their forays into apparent sexual liberation led to emotional devastation. Ostensible sexual freedom untethered from divine truth has shattered families and fractured friendships. Yet our culture, in its movies and television shows, in its popular songs and books, in the examples of stars and politicians, continues to tout sexual "freedom" that is nothing but bondage in disguise. Freedom apart from truth? No way! Freedom brought to us by the truth? Yes! It's the way of Jesus.

Last month I had an experience that helped me grasp the connection between truth and freedom. I accompanied my son, Nathan, on an outing to Six Flags Magic Mountain, a theme park in Southern California. The last time I visited Magic Mountain, about twenty years ago when I was a church high-school director, there were only three roller coasters. At that time the king of all was Colossus. It seemed truly colossal: immense in scale, with fearsome drops and back-wrenching twists. But that was a long time ago, and lots of things at Magic Mountain have changed since then. They've added eight—count 'em, eight—new roller coasters. One of the most recent additions stands adjacent to Colossus. Goliath, as it is aptly called, dwarfs the former king, which now looks like a bowing servant before the towering Goliath. This new coaster features such thrills as a 255-foot, nearly vertical drop, which propels the hapless rider at a speed of eighty-five miles per hour into a pitch-dark tunnel. This is what Nathan calls fun! (I call it sacrificial parenting.)

I did feel a certain delight, I must admit, in hurtling at breakneck speeds hundreds of feet in the air. Although I have a love-hate relationship with roller coasters, I felt exhilarated on Goliath, free to enjoy the ride, free to feel the rush of the wind, free to enjoy the dips and turns, and even to let go of the handles—at least for a moment.

Why did I feel so free? Because I was utterly constrained. The coaster train ran on a meticulously constructed steel track that wasn't going anywhere, thank God and Magic Mountain's engineers. I was restrained in my seat with a steel harness that clamped tightly around my torso. Thus, I was able to experience—and even to enjoy—the freedom of speed and the sense of danger because I wasn't completely free. I was tethered to the train, which was tethered to the track, which was tethered to the ground, all of which were tethered by the truths of natural law.

Our culture has missed the point of freedom by casting off all tethers. It's no wonder that so many people have plunged off the right track and have plummeted into the abyss of moral darkness and personal brokenness. Sure, for a moment untrammeled freedom can offer quite a thrill, but then there's always the fall, and beyond the fall there's always the rock-hard bottom that gladly collects the shattered parts of its victims.

Jesus offers a different freedom, a freedom that gives life rather than taking it, a freedom that leads to wholeness rather than brokenness. He invites us to continue in his truth so that we might experience the most exhilarating freedom of all. "If the Son makes you free," he pledges, "you will be free indeed" (John 8:36, NRSV).

THE FIVE JEWELS OF FREEDOM

What does the true freedom of Jesus include, and what will happen when we experience this freedom? Let me briefly mention five shining gems of Christian freedom.

Freedom with God

As we continue in the word of Jesus, we experience freedom in relationship with God. We will know the truth that we are forgiven through Christ. When we dishonor the Lord through our actions and attitudes, we will confess our sins with confidence, knowing that God "is faithful and just to forgive us and to cleanse us from every wrong" (1 John 1:9). The assurance of this good news will encourage us to stop trying to hide from God. Instead, we will "come boldly to the throne of our gracious God," knowing in advance that "we will receive his mercy, and we will find grace to help us when we need it" (Hebrews 4:16). Coming *boldly* before God's throne—now that's freedom!

Many of us have never known this kind of freedom, even though it has been given to us through Christ. Instead, when we sin we turn away from the Lord, vowing to try harder the next time rather than humbly seeking his forgiveness. Over the years we drift away from God like a swimmer caught in a riptide. The more we thrash away in our attempts to reach the shore of divine love, the more exhausted we become, as we are pulled even farther from our goal. But when we rely upon the revealed truth of God's grace, we will be free to return to God like the prodigal son to his waiting father.

Freedom from the Past

The freedom of Jesus liberates us from the past, from our sins and brokenness. When he encountered the adulterous woman in John 8, Jesus didn't condemn her even though she was guilty of sin. Rather, he set her free to live in a new way, urging her to sin no more. So it is with us. When we placed our faith in Jesus, we died to our old selves, the selves dominated by sin. We were raised to new life, even as Jesus was raised from the dead. In this resurrected reality, everything changes. Pay close attention to Paul's explanation: "What this means is that those who become Christians become new persons. They are not the same anymore, for the old life is gone. A new life has begun!" (2 Corinthians 5:17). In this new life we are no longer dominated by our weaknesses and wounds. The Holy Spirit dwells within us both to heal us and to empower us for living in the full freedom of Christ.

This freedom is not denial or pretending. As Christians we tell the truth about our past. But, unlike so many in our day, we are not dominated by the past. We see ourselves neither as hopelessly sinful people nor as hopelessly wounded victims, but as God's new creations. In this spiritual renewal, even the pain of the past can lead to power for the future.

My friend Shawn has a past like few others. He grew up in a broken, abusive home. Not surprisingly, the wounds of his childhood festered in adolescence, leading Shawn into antisocial behavior. He not only took drugs, but he sold them. He earned respect by fighting better and partying harder than others. By the time he was sixteen, Shawn was on the road to ruin and also, quite literally, to prison. But then he encountered Jesus Christ in a way not unlike the adulterous woman of John 8. He experienced love as never before. Putting his faith in Jesus, Shawn became a new person.

Though his new life was genuine, it didn't instantly transform every aspect of Shawn's nature. The freedom of Christ that begins in conversion grows as we continue in the Word of Jesus. As Shawn walked along the path of true discipleship, he was no longer bound by past failures and injuries. Instead, these became tools for ministry. Shawn felt a calling to help teenagers who were lost in woundedness and sin, just as he had once been. His pain turned to compassion for other broken teenagers. The bonds that once imprisoned Shawn became, through the power of the Spirit, keys to set others free. Now, as a leader in the ministry of Young Life, Shawn influences literally hundreds of kids each year for Christ.

Freedom for Service

Shawn's story also illustrates the third facet of our freedom in Christ: As we continue in the Word of Jesus, we'll be set free for service. Disciples of Jesus live in a peculiar paradox. Though we are free, we choose servanthood. We use our freedom not for our own advantage, but for the sake of others. Peter explained, "You are not slaves; you are free. But your freedom is not an excuse to do evil. You are free to live as God's slaves" (1 Peter 2:16). Free to live as slaves? What sense does that make? Peter alluded to a common experience from the first century to help his original readers understand freedom in Christ. Slavery in the Roman world was not a noble thing, to be sure, but neither was it usually as abusive or as racist as the American system of slavery. Slaves in the first century who earned their freedom often chose to remain slaves of the masters who had treated them graciously. Likewise, though our divine Master has granted us freedom, we "are free to live as God's slaves," knowing that life under his sovereignty is the best life of all. In freedom we choose to serve the Lord.

As servants of God we minister to others. "For you have been called to live in freedom," Paul wrote, "not freedom to satisfy your sinful nature, but freedom to serve one another in love" (Galatians 5:13). The verb rendered here as *serve* literally means "to be a slave." Once again the paradox emerges. We are called to be free people who use our liberty not for ourselves, but for the benefit of others. Because of God's love flowing through us, we freely choose to serve others rather than our own interests. The truth of God's love leads to freedom that leads to serving others in love.

I've seen this pattern reproduced in the lives of hundreds of disciples. The young man who feels he has nothing to offer hears the good news that God has gifted him for ministry. In light of this truth, he begins to teach Sunday school and discovers the joy of helping children grow in faith. The woman who spent most of her Christian life sitting in the pew finally hears the truth that she has been called into ministry. She starts a Bible study for a few friends and rejoices as they begin to grow in their faith. The man who earned big bucks as a successful lawyer retires early so he can invest himself in helping teenagers become disciples of Jesus. And so the story goes, over and over again as God's truth sets people free for the joy of service.

I do not mean to imply, however, that Christian service always leads to happiness this side of heaven. Throughout this book I've mentioned unfortunate situations from my own ministry when I faced criticism or discouragement. My experience isn't unique, I'm sad to say. But when I remember that my service is primarily for God, then I'm encouraged to keep on serving even when the going is tough.

God's truth also sets us free from the insidious idea that we are simply too busy to spend time serving him. The world tells us that what matters most in life is what we gain for ourselves: financial prosperity, social esteem, physical beauty, sexual pleasure. When we're investing all of our time in such pursuits, we don't have anything left for service. But divine truth helps us rethink our fundamental values. In the light of Scripture, we see the emptiness of mindless entertainment and selfish gain. We realize that serving the Lord is not something trivial and meaningless, but essential and profoundly gratifying. The truth sets us free to discover not just the value of service but also its sublime joy.

During my tenure as a senior pastor, I have watched with gratitude as people of worldly success and influence make Christian service a top priority. A man who runs a billion-dollar company is a faithful deacon, caring and praying for the personal needs of his flock. Another man who regularly gives speeches to thousands of people throughout the country teaches my daughter's Sunday-school class. When I ask him why he makes time for this, his answer is telling: "There's nothing more important than teaching Sunday school." God's truth has set him free to serve.

Freedom with Others

The fourth facet of freedom comes in our relationships with other people. What keeps us from being who we truly are with those around us? Why do we so often hide behind a mask? The simple answer is fear. We are afraid that if we let others see us as we are, they will criticize us or laugh at us or even reject us. So we hide our weaknesses, our woundedness, our sins. We aren't free to be ourselves, even with our dearest friends and family members.

Jesus wants to change all of that. The same forgiveness that leads to freedom with God touches our human relationships as well. Remember how Jesus teaches us to ask for forgiveness: "[F]orgive us our sins, just as we have forgiven those who have sinned against us" (Matthew 6:12). Did you catch that? We ask God to forgive us *just as* we have forgiven others. Divine forgiveness and human forgiveness are interwoven like threads in a fine tapestry. To ensure that we don't miss this crucial point, two verses later Jesus explained further: "If you forgive those who sin against you, your heavenly Father will forgive you. But if you refuse to forgive others, your Father will not forgive your sins" (verses 14-15). What an astounding teaching! If we are stingy in mutual forgiveness, then God will be stingy in forgiving us. If we are generous, then God will be so with us.

If we live in a community of Jesus' disciples who are continuing in his Word, then we will experience unprecedented freedom in relationship with one another. Not only will we forgive each other, but we also will love each other as Jesus has loved us. We will serve one another in imitation of Jesus, the One who "came here not to be served but to serve others, and to give [his] life as a ransom for many" (Mark 10:45). We will "share each other's troubles and problems, and in this way obey the law of Christ" (Galatians 6:2). We will "rejoice with those who rejoice" and "weep with those who weep" (Romans 12:15, NRSV). In such a community of disciples, we will experience freedom to be authentic, to share our victories and our defeats, our dreams and our fears, our strengths and our wounds.

Rather than enjoying the freedom of Christian fellowship, many of us live instead like Jean Valjean, the protagonist in Victor Hugo's novel *Les Misérables*.[5] As a young man, Valjean stole a loaf of bread to feed his starving family. Caught by the authorities, he squandered almost twenty years in the foul prisons of nineteenth-century France. When he finally secured his release, he was forced to endure the shame of an ex-con. In desperation, Valjean adopted a new identity, ultimately achieving both financial and social success.

Yet he wasn't free. On the one hand, he was hunted by Javert, the unyielding agent of cruel French law who had sworn to return Valjean to prison. On the other hand, Valjean was pursued by his own relentless shame. He could not share his true identity even with those who loved him unconditionally. Though no longer bound within a French prison, Valjean was hardly free.

I know many Christians who, though delivered from the wages of sin, nevertheless live like Jean Valjean. I think of a woman who for years struggled in a horrendous marriage to an adulterous husband. Her greatest fear was that people in her church would find out. As a pastor I am often frustrated by the reticence of my people to share with others that for which they most need support and prayer. The father whose son is a drug addict aches inside but keeps his anguish to himself because he's afraid of looking bad. The student on the verge of failing chemistry doesn't ask for prayer because she's too embarrassed.

Jesus invites us into a qualitatively different sort of community, a place of freedom forged by God's grace. I realize, of course, that churches fall short of this ideal. Christian communities can major in judgment rather than mercy. For this reason, we must show discretion when we share ourselves with others, making sure those to whom we open our hearts are trustworthy and kind. As we continue in the Word of Jesus, as we are molded by divine truth, we will experience increasing freedom both to be authentic and to accept others with the same grace that God has extended to us.

Freedom to Live Truthfully

The fifth facet of Christian freedom both stems from and leads to the truth. The more we embrace God's truth, the more we'll be set free to live truthfully. No longer will we be slaves to image, to the approval of others, or to the entrapments of deception and spin. We'll be free to say what we believe as well as to be who we are.

I first observed the relentless, voracious appetite of deceit while in college. One of my roommates began falling behind in his schoolwork. Rather than honestly explaining his predicament to his professors, Mike wove a complex web of deceit. He told one professor that he couldn't finish his work because of a family crisis. With another he claimed physical illness as his excuse. And so forth. Though Mike's multiple deceptions did buy him a bit more time for academic production, they consumed his soul. He was always wary, fearful that one of his lies might fail or that he might forget which untruth he had told to which professor. He couldn't even answer the phone because he had told one instructor that he was out of town on personal business. Deception devoured Mike's peace of mind.

Although most of us don't go to such extremes, we know what it's like to hide our true selves and to live for the elusive approval of others. Early in my ministry at Irvine Presbyterian, I preached a series of sermons that called for costly discipleship. Although many church members affirmed my preaching, one couple wrote a scathing, secret letter to the board of elders, which was read aloud in the biweekly board meeting. The letter accused me of preaching legalism rather than the gospel. I was horrified when, in response to this letter, two of the more outspoken elders agreed, while others were strangely silent. Confused and discouraged, I began to second-guess my preaching. Perhaps I'd been too blunt about what Christian discipleship entails. Perhaps I should have been a little less truthful and tried harder to assuage the guilty feelings of my congregation. In my desire for their approval, I considered drifting from the path of complete honesty and instead soft-pedaling the call of Jesus to take up the cross daily and follow him.

As I drove to church on the Sunday morning following the board meeting, my heart was tied up in knots. What if my preaching cost me my job? How could I preach to my congregation that morning, knowing that some people disapproved of me and what I was saying? In desperation I called out to God for help.

Suddenly everything became clear. God had called me to preach his truth, no matter what. My sermon that morning, although intended for the ears of my flock, was really an offering to the Lord. What mattered most was not the approval of people, but of God. "Lord, this sermon is a gift for you," I prayed.

"I will seek to honor you in all that I say, no matter what happens. You have called me, and my heart's deepest desire is your glory. Help me, Lord, to preach your truth." And so he did. As I began to preach that morning, the fact of God's call upon my life and his persistent love for me set me free to tell the truth.

This kind of freedom isn't only for preachers. A couple of years ago a man in my congregation sold his business in order to run for political office. He wanted to invest his life in making a difference in the world. Though it was John's first political campaign, he won the election handily. His introduction to California politics wasn't altogether friendly, however. As he began to serve in his elected capacity, he soon found himself in trouble with powerful political operatives. How did he get into this fix? By telling the truth as he saw it, rejecting the "make nice" compromises of political expediency. Before long John faced a stark decision, either to continue to speak truthfully and put his political future at risk or to bend the truth and become "one of the boys."

When I met with John, he had decided which course to take, but he wanted some pastoral encouragement. "If I stick with the truth," he explained, "it might very well be the end of my career in politics. But I need to do what's right and leave the results to the Lord." John's confidence in God gave him the strength to uphold the truth. The fact of God's sovereignty and love emboldened him to be truthful in an arena where, sadly, truth is so often lacking.

If you have put your trust in Jesus Christ, then you are a beloved child of God. The bedrock truth of God's love for you will give you the freedom to speak and to live the truth no matter what the consequences. The truth of God's mercy will set you free from the fear of failure. The truth of God's sovereignty will reassure you that your life, not to mention all of human history, is in God's gracious hands.

The path of truthfulness is the narrow path in today's world, by far the road less traveled. But it is the way of God, the way of significance, the way of freedom. If you continue in the Word of Christ, then you will be his genuine disciple. You will know the truth, and the truth will set you free—free to be intimate with God, free from the constraints of your past, free to give yourself away to others in Christlike service, free to share your life with others, free to speak truthfully so that the light of God might shine into the darkness of this world.

As a young boy, when I faced situations that challenged my honesty, my mother would often say, "Mark, just tell the truth." Her simple, straightforward advice remains as valid today as it was forty years ago. So allow me to pass on my mother's wisdom to you: "Just tell the truth." But, let me add, do more than tell it. Let the truth fill your heart, transform your mind, and come alive in your actions. When you feel tempted to twist the truth or leave it behind altogether, remember the sage words of George Herbert: "Dare to be true."

May God, the Truthful Trinity,
grant you the wisdom and courage to live truthfully!
To him be all the glory!

QUESTIONS FOR STUDY
AND GROWTH

DARE TO BE TRUE TODAY

This discussion guide is designed for a variety of uses: personal reflection, discussion with a prayer partner, small-group study, or Christian education in a local church setting. The questions for each chapter vary in their focus. Some relate directly to the content of the chapter. Others are more wide ranging. Many of the questions are meant to help you relate the material of the chapter to your own life in a practical way.

For further study you may wish to examine more closely the Scripture passages that are highlighted in each chapter.

INTRODUCTION: DO YOU DARE?

1. In what recent situations, if any, were you not completely honest? Did you lie or did you merely "spin" the truth? What were your motivations?

2. Does an uncompromising commitment to truthful living mean that you must say *everything* that comes into your head? Why or why not?

3. In what kinds of situations is lying the easier course of action? Why? When have you found it especially difficult to tell the truth?

4. What impact does spin have on our society? What effect does it have on you?

5. When have you been hurt by lying, either as the liar or as the victim? Did you experience reconciliation? Explain.

6. Do you think truthfulness requires daring? Why or why not?

7. Whom do you consider to be especially truthful? Think about people in your own life as well as public figures.

CHAPTER 1: THE TRUTHFUL TRINITY

1. When, if ever, have you found yourself in a situation like that of Ted, speaking unwisely about something without realizing to whom you were speaking? What was the outcome?

2. When you think of the Trinity—Father, Son, and Holy Spirit— which member do you usually associate with truth? Why?

3. The Bible emphasizes the close connection between truth and trust. When have you experienced the inseparability of these two qualities?

4. Do you sometimes struggle to trust God's revealed truth? If so, when and why?

5. What circumstances in your life make trusting God more difficult?

6. How can we have confidence in the truth and yet be humble as we speak of it to others?

7. When, if ever, have you felt unsettled by the secular understanding of truth? When has this been an issue for you? How did you resolve the conflict between the culture's view and Scripture's definition of truth?

8. How do you respond to the fact that the God of truth seeks you?

9. Do you think of worship as necessarily being centered in truth? Why or why not? In what ways does your experience of worship impact your theology?

CHAPTER 2: CALLED TO TRUTHFULNESS

1. When, if ever, have you found yourself in a situation like that of the
    pseudo-survey where it seemed that everyone else was willing to go
    along with deception? What did you do in response to the situation?
    Why?

2. Which contemporary teachers, philosophers, or gurus remind you of
    the first-century Sophists? What are the primary similarities?

3. Why did Paul reveal such personal information in 2 Corinthians? Do
    you think religious leaders today should be that open about their per-
    sonal struggles? Why or why not? Are there certain struggles that a
    leader should not share with his or her congregation?

4. In what ways does the church function as a pillar of truth in our
    society today?

5. In what circumstances are you tempted to exaggerate to the point of lying? What makes exaggeration so tempting in those circumstances?

6. If people are sick of spin, why is it still so prevalent in our world?

7. If you had been in Sherron Watkins's place at Enron, what would you have thought and felt about your options? Do you think you would have written the memo to Kenneth Lay? Why or why not?

8. Where in your life do you find it hard to be truth-full?

CHAPTER 3: SPURNING SPIN

1. Before reading this chapter, did you know that the story of George Washington and the cherry tree was fictional? If not, how did you feel when you realized that you had been duped by Parson Weems? What does this example suggest about the power of truth and falsehood?

2. Which of the three steps in spurning spin do you find to be the trickiest: making a commitment, recognizing deception, or rejecting deception? Explain.

3. In which situations is a deception or some type of lie morally acceptable? Why do you think it's okay in such a setting?

4. Consider the three common contexts for spin that are mentioned in chapter 3: Perjured Promotion, Avoiding Accountability, Traffic and Tardiness. In which of these areas, if any, do you struggle with truthfulness? What leads to this struggle?

5. Where else in everyday life do you find it especially tough to tell the full truth? What makes this area (or these areas) such a struggle?

6. Have you ever had an experience in which one person's honesty, like Steve's, transformed the dynamic of a group's interactions? What was the outcome?

7. If you were in Abraham Lincoln's shoes, would you have gone to that much trouble to return a few pennies? Why or why not? If your answer is no, what would you have done instead?

CHAPTER 4: FACING THE TRUTH WE'D RATHER AVOID

1. When you sin but don't want to admit your culpability, whom do you tend to blame? Your spouse? Your parents? Society? The church? Some other person or institution? Circumstances?

2. Given the Bible's clear statement of God's mercy and the promise of divine forgiveness through Christ, why do we nevertheless balk at confessing our sins? What can help us overcome these hesitations?

3. How do you respond to the idea that God is seeking you like a Shepherd looking for a lost sheep or a Father running to embrace his long-lost child?

4. When have you experienced the cleansing and new life that follows truthful confession? What effect did that have on your life and your outlook?

5. James 5:16 says, "Confess your sins to each other and pray for each other so that you may be healed." Have you ever done this? Why or why not? Why does confession to another person help us experience divine healing?

6. In what ways, if any, does your church encourage honest confession of sin? What are the explicit and implicit messages about confession that your church gives?

7. When did you last spend extended time in confession? Is it time for you to do so again?

Chapter 5: Divine Training in Truthfulness

1. When, if ever, have you tried to learn something from an expert who couldn't teach the subject? What do you think kept this person from being an effective teacher?

2. God is the Supreme Expert on truth. What makes him such an effective teacher of truthfulness?

3. As you think about your own life, what or who has taught you to be truthful?

4. Have you ever been caught in a lie or other deception and learned the hard way that "dishonesty doesn't pay"? If so, in what ways did your words and behavior change after that incident?

5. When, if ever, have you received the Holy Spirit's help when you were seeking to be completely honest? What about help from the church? How did that help change you?

6. What keeps you from sitting at the feet of the Master of truth? What can you do to remove those barriers?

CHAPTER 6: TRUTHFUL COMMUNITY

1. What social pressures push you in the direction of lying?

2. In what ways is your experience of Christian community anything like what Jesus described in John 17? How does your experience differ from Jesus' description?

3. In what ways, if any, has belonging to a Christian community helped you become more honest?

4. Think about your own Christian community (church, fellowship group, accountability group). Evaluate its strengths and weaknesses in light of the dimensions of truthful community—encouraging truthfulness, modeling truthfulness, discerning the truth, members sharing the truth about themselves, others telling us the truth about ourselves.

5. What could you do to help your Christian community become more truth-filled?

6. How often do you hear the truth of the gospel in your church? In what ways is this truth communicated? What difference does it make in your life?

7. What people in your life need to hear the good news of God's love for them in Christ? How might you share this good news with them? What, specifically, could you say?

CHAPTER 7: SPEAK GENTLY AND BURY YOUR BIG STICK

1. Describe a time, if any, when you heard a person speaking the truth, but in a tone that made you want to disagree with him or her.

2. When, if ever, have you been arrogant or too strident in expressing the truth? What kept you from using a more gentle tone?

3. Is boldness in truth-speaking inconsistent with gentleness? Why or why not? How can we be both courageous and humble?

4. God's truth runs counter to the world's system. How can we find the strength to be gentle when others are opposing the truth?

5. How do you feel about personal confrontation? Have you ever been confronted in love by someone? How did you react? Have you ever been the one to do the confronting? What did you learn from this experience?

6. When is it acceptable for Christians to raise their voices? When is it wrong to do so? How can we tell the difference?

7. Why do you think we tend to confuse gentleness with wimpishness? What is the difference between the two?

8. Whom do you know who succeeds at speaking the truth plainly but gently?

9. If you're not a humble person, what can you do about it? What steps can you take to become humble?

CHAPTER 8: TRUTH IN THE TRENCHES

1. Describe a time in your adult life when you found it extremely difficult to tell the truth. What made it so difficult? What did you end up doing?

2. What factors in your everyday life make truth telling hard? Describe some situations that fit the three primary challenges: content, context, consequences.

3. What helps you to be truthful? Chapter 8 suggests five aids: commandment, commitment, counsel of Scripture, Counselor, community. Which of these matters most to you on a daily basis? Which of these matters most when you're facing a tough challenge? Explain.

4. When have you sensed strongly that truthfulness is at the center of the spiritual battle in which we find ourselves?

5. How do you "speak the truth in love"? When, if ever, have you chosen to be silent rather than speak out of love? How can you tell if truth speaking is done in love or not?

6. Have you made an intentional, expressed commitment to truthfulness? Explain. Are there people in your life who know about this commitment and who can help hold you accountable? If so, who?

CHAPTER 9: TRUTH WITH FEET

1. Whom do you know who exemplifies "walking the walk" (i.e., people whose truthful speech is matched by truthful living)?

2. How often are you tempted to pursue a path that is inconsistent with what you tell others? What do you do in the face of these temptations?

3. In what ways has Scripture helped you live in a manner consistent with the truth?

4. Are you living in close relationship with other Christians who are your partners in the walk of truth? If not, what might you do to remedy this situation?

5. When, if ever, have you experienced the freedom that comes when you lower your mask and stop hiding who you really are? How did this freedom enrich your life and relationships?

6. What keeps you from being yourself when you're around those who love you?

7. In what part of your life would you like God to help you walk according to the truth? Explain.

Chapter 10: Living as Children of Light

1. How does it feel to be a child of the light in the midst of a dark world? In what situations do you notice the contrast most vividly?

2. Do you ever feel alienated from the world because you're a person of light? Explain.

3. In what ways does your light shine in the darkness around you?

4. Many of us draw back from "exposing the unfruitful works of darkness." Why do you think that's the case? What are we afraid of?

5. In what ways are you inviting others into the light of Christ? Why is this so important? If you're not doing this, why not?

6. How might you be more effective in this ministry of invitation?

7. When, if ever, have you seen people drawn to Christ because of the truthfulness of his people? What was the truth that had such power?

8. How might you shine more brightly in your part of the world?

CHAPTER 11: ENJOY THE FREEDOM OF TRUTH

1. Do you feel free to share your personal struggles with others? Why or why not?

2. Describe a time, if any, when you wished you could just "be yourself" and stop trying to impress others or earn their approval. Why did you feel this so keenly?

3. Why do you think truth and freedom are so intertwined in Scripture?

4. Do you tend to think of freedom as something that comes from truth or as something that is independent of the constraints of truth? Explain.

5. Think about the illustration of the roller coaster. In what other life situations is freedom tethered to some reliable foundation?

6. Chapter 11 lists five "gems" of freedom: freedom with God, freedom from the past, freedom for service, freedom with others, freedom to live truthfully. Which of these freedoms do you most enjoy today? Which do you long to experience more deeply? Explain.

7. Are you ready to "dare to be true"? What, if anything, is holding you back? What encourages you to step out with a new commitment to live in complete honesty?

NOTES

Introduction

1. Excerpts from this interview are found in Bill Hoffmann, "Lying's Great, Says Lizzie Pal," *New York Post,* 22 February 2002.

2. The study by Colorado-based Avert, Inc., was reviewed in Jeffrey Kluger, "Pumping Up Your Past," *Time,* 10 June 2002. Also found at www. time.com/ time/magazine/article/ 0,9171,1101020610-257116,00.html.

3. Katy Abel, Family Education Network, "New Survey: 7 in 10 Teens Admit School Cheating," review of survey statistics in "Report Card on the Ethics of American Youth" by Josephson Institute of Ethics. Found at www.familyeducation.com/article/0,1120,1-19468,00.html.

4. Dr. Robert Burton, "Docs Who Lie and the Patients Who Thank Them," *Salon.com,* 1 November 1999. Found at www.salon.com/ health/col/bob/ 1999/11/01/dr_bob/index1.html.

5. The study by Professor Robert Feldman of the University of Massachusetts was summarized in a press release by EurekAlert! on 10 June 2002: "Umass Researcher Finds Most People Lie in Everyday Conversation." Found at www.eurekalert.org/pub_releases/2002-06/uoma-urf061002.php.

6. Bill Press, *Spin This! All the Ways We Don't Tell the Truth* (New York: Pocket Books, 2001), xiv.

7. For an extended discussion, see Sissela Bok, *Lying: Moral Choice in Public and Private Life,* 2d ed. (New York: Vintage, 1999), 20-8.

8. This information comes from an NPR-Kaiser-Kennedy School poll, "Attitudes Toward Government." It is based on a phone survey of more than fifteen hundred people conducted May 26–June 25, 2000. In this survey, only 29 percent of people claimed to trust the federal government at least most of the time. Eighty percent of the respondents cited the dishonesty of leaders in getting elected as a reason for distrusting the government. The survey results can be found at www.npr.org/programs/specials/poll/govt/gov.toplines.pdf.

   Cynicism goes hand-in-hand with the loss of trust. Another survey found that 71 percent of Americans believe that "politics in America is generally pretty disgusting." The major reason? Spin, once again. This survey was conducted March 1–5, 2000, by The Joan Shorenstein Center on the Press, Politics and Public Policy of the John F. Kennedy School of Government at Harvard University. Further information can be found at www.vanishingvoter.org/releases/ 03-13-00.shtml.

Moreover, according to William Chaloupka, "We are now living in the midst of the most cynical era in American history." (From book jacket of *Everybody Knows: Cynicism in America* [Minneapolis: University of Minnesota Press, 1999]). Given the epidemic of spin throughout our land, this conclusion comes as no surprise.

9. Jim Eskin, "The Truth Speaks Louder than PR Spin," *San Antonio Business Journal,* 26 October 1998. Found at http://sanantonio.bizjournals.com/ sanantonio/stories/1998/10/26/editorial2.html.

10. Larry B. Stammer, "Organized Religion Slips in Survey," *Los Angeles Times,* 11 January 2003. Found at http://pqasb.pqarchiver.com/latimes.

11. Bok, *Lying,* 25.

12. George Herbert, "The Church Porch," stanza 13, *The Temple* (Cambridge: Thom. Buck, 1633), 3. Facsimile edition published by The Scholar Press Limited, Menston, England, 1968. Spelling of words updated. Emphasis added.

Chapter 1

1. See John 15:26.

2. In Deuteronomy 32:4, for example, where the *King James Version* has the phrase "God of *truth,*" both the *New International Version* and the *New Revised Standard Version* use *"faithful* God." God speaks truth, and he is also true to us, or completely faithful in all his dealings. In Psalm 31:5, the *New International Version* employs "God of *truth,*" whereas the *New Living Translation* and the *New Revised Standard Version* read *"faithful* God."

3. Francis Brown, S. R. Driver, and Charles A. Briggs, *A Hebrew and English Lexicon of the Old Testament* (Oxford: Clarendon Press, 1979), s.v. *'emet.*

4. See, for example, Genesis 42:16; 1 Kings 10:6; 2 Kings 20:3.

5. See especially John 17:13-21.

6. John Calvin, *Institutes of the Christian Religion: A New Translation by Henry Beveridge* (Grand Rapids: Eerdmans, 1995), 2.2.15. Electronic text hypertexted and prepared by OakTree Software Specialists.

7. See Luke 15:3-32. See also Genesis 3, where God seeks the man and the woman even after they sin.

8. I have explored the different dimensions of fellowship with God in my book *After "I Believe": Experiencing Authentic Christian Living* (Grand Rapids: Baker, 2002).

Chapter 2

1. For a discussion of the Sophists and other wandering philosophers in the first century A.D., see Ben Witherington III, *Conflict and Community in Corinth: A Socio-Rhetorical Commentary on 1 and 2 Corinthians* (Grand Rapids: Eerdmans, 1995), 348-50; Abraham Malherbe, *Paul and the Popular Philosophers* (Minneapolis: Fortress, 1989), 35-48; and Bruce W. Winter, *Philo and Paul among the Sophists* (Cambridge: Cambridge University Press, 1997).

2. This is a literal translation of the phrase in 2 Corinthians 4:2 rendered in the *New Living Translation* as "We tell the truth before God."

3. See 2 Corinthians 11:23-25; 12:7-10.

4. George Herbert, "The Church Porch," stanza 13, *The Temple* (Cambridge: Thom. Buck, 1633), 3. Facsimile edition published by The Scholar Press Limited, Menston, England, 1968. Spelling of words updated. Emphasis added.

5. See Matthew 5:14-16.

6. See John 17:17-18.

7. Abraham McLaughlin, "In Age of Spin, Voters Yearn for the Blunt," *Christian Science Monitor,* 4 February 2000. Found at www.csmonitor. com/cgi-bin/getasciiarchive?script/2000/02/04/p1s5.txt.

8. Michael Richards, "No More Truth, Just Spin," *The Daily Illini Online,* 17 January 2001. Found at www.dailyillini.com/jan01/jan17/opinions/col01.shtml.

9. Quotation by Karenna Gore Schiff, the daughter of former Vice President Al Gore. In Katherine Pfleger, "Candidates Failing to Woo Young Voters," *Detroit News,* 5 November 2000. Found at http://detnews.com/2000/politics/0011/05/a21-143765.htm.

10. Excerpts from letters to the British Broadcasting Corporation. *BBC News: Talking Point,* 13 June 2000. Found at http://news.bbc.co.uk/2/hi/talking_point/782684.stm.

11. From *TheSchoolQuarterly.com* electronic bulletin board in New Zealand. Found at www.theschoolquarterly.com/discus/discussion_stalbans/000000e7.htm.

12. Quotation by Sherron Watkins from her letter to Kenneth Lay dated August 15, 2001, released by the House Energy and Commerce Committee. Found at http://energycommerce.house.gov/107/hearings/ 02142002Hearing489/tab10.pdf.

13. Jack Modesett, quoted in Bob Jones, "Reluctant Hero," *World Magazine,* 2 February 2002, emphasis added. Found at www.worldmag. com/world/issue/02-02-02/national_3.asp.

14. *Time,* 30 December 2002.

15. Aleksandr Solzhenitsyn, "Nobel Lecture on Literature," trans. F. D. Reeve (New York: Farrar, Straus and Giroux, 1972). Digital formatting by The Augustine Club at Columbia University, 1999.

Chapter 3

1. From Mason Locke Weems, *A History of the Life and Death, Virtues and Exploits of General George Washington.* Originally published in 1800. Found at http://xroads.Virginia.edu/~CAP/gw/chap1.html. A helpful discussion of Parson Weems and his time can be found in Daniel J. Boorstin, *The Americans: The National Experience* (New York: Random House, Vintage, 1965), 340-5. It appears that Weems actually plagiarized the story of the cherry tree from the English writer Dr. James Beattie; see David Nyberg, *The Varnished Truth* (Chicago: The University of Chicago Press, 1994), 154-5.

2. Professor Robert Feldman, University of Massachusetts, EurekAlert! press release, 10 June 2002: "Umass Researcher Finds Most People Lie in Everyday Conversation." Found at www.eurekalert.org/pub_releases/ 2002-06/ uoma-urf061002.php.

3. The ninth commandment focuses specifically on behavior in a judicial context—giving testimony in a court of law. But its implications for a broader range of truthfulness are obvious.

4. Edmund Morris, *Dutch: A Memoir of Ronald Reagan* (New York: Random House, 1999). See the article by Josh Tyrangiel, "A History of His Own Making," *Time,* 24 June 2001. Found at www.time.com/time/ education/article/ 0,8599,165156,00.html.

5. Edmund Morris, "Just Our Imaginations, Running Away," *New York Times,* 22 June 2001.

6. I refer again to a study that found 44 percent of 2.6 million job applicants had doctored their résumés by adding lies. The study by Colorado-based Avert, Inc., was reviewed in Jeffrey Kluger, "Pumping Up Your Past," *Time,* 10 June 2002. Found at www.time.com/time/magazine/article/ 0,9171,1101020610-257116,00.html.

7. For more on this, see Charles J. Sykes, *A Nation of Victims: The Decay of the American Character* (New York: St. Martin's Press, 1992).

8. Unlike the story of George Washington and the cherry tree, which is well known to be fictitious, the story of Lincoln's long walk to return a small amount of money is taken by many historians to be true—or based upon the truth, at any rate. Yet the story is often exaggerated in the extreme. I came across versions where Lincoln walked twenty miles to return a penny or ten miles through the snow to do his honest deed. For a responsible investigation of Lincoln's legendary honesty, see Kenneth J. Winkle, *The Young Eagle: The Rise of Abraham Lincoln* (Dallas: Taylor Trade Publications, 2001).

9. See the account in Stephen B. Oates, *With Malice Toward None: A Life of Abraham Lincoln* (New York: HarperPerennial, 1994). I am grateful to Ron White for bringing this story to my attention.

Chapter 4

1. Commentary on Genesis 3:12 from John Calvin, *Calvin's Commentary* (partial), trans. John King, M.D. (Genesis) and John Owen (Minor Prophets and Hebrews). Electronic text hypertexted and prepared by OakTree Software Specialists. Emphasis added.
2. Calvin, *Calvin's Commentary*.
3. A paraphrase of Psalm 51:7.

Chapter 5

1. W. V. Quine, *Philosophy of Logic* (Englewood Cliffs, N.J.: Prentice-Hall, 1970), 14.
2. I am grateful to my church's junior-high director, Ryan Nielsen, for bringing this story to my attention. It circulates on the Internet and elsewhere in a variety of forms. Its essential truth has been confirmed by Professor Bonk, though he acknowledges that it has been embellished by certain legendary accretions. A member of my church actually took this professor's introductory chemistry course at Duke University and says Professor Bonk told this story in class to encourage students to be honest. For an analysis of the veracity of the account, see www.snopes. com/college/exam/flattire.htm. This Web site is a goldmine for people who are trying to evaluate the truth or falsehood of so-called urban legends.

Chapter 6

1. See EurekAlert! 10 June 2002: "Umass Researcher Finds Most People Lie in Everyday Conversation." Found at www.eurekalert.org/pub_ releases/2002-06/uoma-urf061002.php.
2. "Introduction: What's Going on Here?" in *The Truth About the Truth: De-confusing and Re-constructing the Postmodern World,* ed. Walter Truett Anderson (New York: Penguin Putnam, Tarcher, 1995), 8.
3. For more theological and practical input on living in authentic Christian community, see my book *After "I Believe": Experiencing Authentic Christian Living* (Grand Rapids: Baker, 2002).

Chapter 7

1. See Galatians 5:22-23.

2. Charles Dickens, *David Copperfield* (1850; reprint, New York: Modern Library, 2000).

3. The text of Mother Teresa's speech can be found in "Mother Teresa Goes to Washington," available at the Catholic Educator's Resource Center. Found at http://catholiceducation.org/articles/abortion/ ab0039.html.

4. Former presidential speech writer Peggy Noonan wrote a moving report of Mother Teresa's speech. See "Still, Small Voice," *Crisis* 16, no. 2 (February 1998): 12-7. This article is also available at the Catholic Educator's Resource Center at http://catholiceducation.org/articles/ catholic_stories/cs0004.html.

5. See 1 Peter 3:17-18; 4:12-13.

6. In addition to biblical passages already mentioned in this chapter, I think of Proverbs 15:1, which says: "A gentle answer turns away wrath, but harsh words stir up anger" and 15:4, "Gentle words bring life and health; a deceitful tongue crushes the spirit."

7. Abraham Lincoln, "The Second Inaugural," quoted in Ronald C. White Jr., *Lincoln's Greatest Speech: The Second Inaugural* (New York: Simon & Schuster, 2002), 18-9.

8. White, *Lincoln's Greatest Speech,* 202.

Chapter 8

1. Katherine Stroup, "Kids, Are We Having Fun Yet?" *Newsweek,* 8 July 2002, 61.

2. Sissela Bok, *Lying: Moral Choice in Public and Private Life,* 2d ed. (New York: Vintage, 1999), 23.

3. Kris Frieswick, "Liar, Liar," *CFO Magazine,* December 2002. Found at www.cfo.com/article/1,5309,8237%7C%7CM%7C446,00.html.

4. From the movie *Liar, Liar,* directed by Tom Shadyac, screenplay by Paul Guay and Stephen Mazur, Universal Pictures, 1997.

5. Martin Luther, "A Mighty Fortress Is Our God," trans. Frederick H. Hedge, 1852. Public domain.

Chapter 9

1. I have explored the relationship of Christian faith and Christian community in my book *After "I Believe": Experiencing Authentic Christian Living* (Grand Rapids: Baker, 2002).

2. *The Mask,* directed by Charles Russell, screenplay by Mike Werb, New Line Studios, 1994.

Chapter 10

1. Quotations from *The Rule of the Community,* a foundational guide for the Jewish community at Qumran. Florentino García Martínez, *The Dead Sea Scrolls Translated: The Qumran Texts in English,* 2d ed. (Grand Rapids: Eerdmans, 1996), 1QS III 20-21; II 24; III 13; IV 5.

2. 1QS V 1-2, emphasis added.

3. 1QS V 10-11, emphasis added.

4. J. R. R. Tolkien, *The Lord of the Rings* (Boston: Houghton Mifflin, 1994), 566.

5. 1QS I 9-10; IV 17; 1QM I 1-8.

6. See the cover of *Time,* 30 December 2002.

Chapter 11

1. For more on this idea, see my book *Jesus Revealed* (Colorado Springs: Water-Brook, 2002).

2. Jessica Burns, "The Double Life of Catherine M," *The Observer,* 19 May 2002. Found at www.observer.co.uk/magazine/story/ 0,11913,718035,00.html.

3. Susannah Meadows, "Memoirs of a Bare Naked Lady," *Newsweek,* 27 May 2002.

4. From *Redemptor Hominis* (1979), quoted in Avery Dulles, "John Paul II and the Truth about Freedom," *First Things* 55 (August/September 1995): 36-41. Found at www.firstthings.com/ftissues/ft9508/articles/ dulles.html.

5. Victor Hugo, *Les Misérables,* trans. Norman Denny (original French edition; 1862; reprint, New York: Penguin, 1998).